The Young Wizard's Hexopedia:
A Guide to Magical Words & Phrases

By Anthemion Deckle Buckram, the Lettered

Rediscovered by Craig Conley, Antiquary

Saint Augustine

Contents

How To Use This Book

Once you plunge into the world of magic words and develop your inborn powers, you'll have no trouble finding ways to use them. (Just think of all the times in the past when you *wished* you had some magic words at your disposal!) Meanwhile, here are just a few of the infinite examples of ways you can use this book:

* To travel through time.
* To undo a bad haircut.
* To stop a poisoned arrow flying toward your heart.
* To help a spider reach the top of a table.
* To hide something embarrassing.
* To prop open a door.
* To illuminate the darkness.
* To find lost tennis balls.
* To change the flavors of foodstuffs.
* To remember to bring that thing with you next time.
* To invent a new musical instrument.
* To play card games with your animal familiars.
* To speak in slow motion.
* To find the answer to the question. (Yes, *that* question.)

Most of all, allow this book to be a ball of light in your hand.

Introduction

An entire book full of magic words! In your very hands!

It's a bit overwhelming, isn't it?

Sometimes when you hold something precious and exquisite, you don't even know where to begin in your exploration of its dazzling fascination. You don't know how to *start* observing it and making it yours. And *can* it really be yours? you ask yourself. Has it fallen into your hands through some sort of bizarre mistake?

Here is the first secret of many to come:
You are worthy of holding this book.

And here's the second secret:
Begin anywhere you like.

The story of magic words, what they're made of, where they came from, where they take you, how 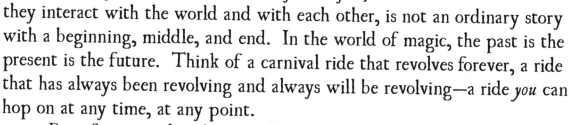 they interact with the world and with each other, is not an ordinary story with a beginning, middle, and end. In the world of magic, the past is the present is the future. Think of a carnival ride that revolves forever, a ride that has always been revolving and always will be revolving—a ride *you* can hop on at any time, at any point.

But of course it's only natural you should want to know, in a general way, what you can expect from this magical ride (though the specifics will be determined only by your own imagination and dedication).

Expect magic speaking, writing, and listening. *Expect* a treasure chest of techniques to access the full wisdom and power of the magic. *Expect* spells for beginning things, for attracting things, for protecting things, and for bestowing things.

The very fact that you have picked this book up strongly suggests that you are a wizardly individual. Your answers to a few simple questions can serve to confirm this:

Have you ever wished for something that came true?
Wizards are gifted at harnessing the power of thoughts.

Have you ever not spoken something you were thinking, for fear of its effect?

Wizards are very sensitive to the power of words.

Have you ever gazed into a crackling fire and found your mind drifting into a relaxed state?

The art of mental relaxation is essential to wizardry.

Have you ever had the feeling that an animal could understand what you were telling it?

Wizards have the power to communicate with other creatures.

Have you ever detected a hidden meaning in a sentence?

Wizards can see beyond the surface.

Have you ever played a word game?

Wizards have a knack for manipulating language for magical effect.

Have you ever dreamed you could fly?

Wizards aspire to what others think impossible.

If you've answered yes to some or all of these questions, you have the creative, inquisitive, imaginative, and analytical mind of a wizard. You have a mind that's ready to learn to speak magically and more magically . . . to assemble, paint, and manipulate words, even invisible words . . . to become fluent in the language, or rather *languages*, of spellcraft . . . to interact on a magical level with the elements, the animals, and the trees.

Are you ready to begin?

We know you've opened this book at a moment when you're supposed to be doing something else. But you'll get to it later, as we both know it's something that can wait a bit. You deserve this moment to yourself, to satisfy a curiosity that has been slowly growing in the back of your mind. Relax, for we* understand you.

That curiosity of yours is in fact shrouded by the ghost of a doubt. You wonder whether the age of magic words has passed. After all, even your own words sometimes fail you, while other people rarely say what they mean or mean what they say. (Oh, yes, we've noticed it too.) We understand your concerns, better than you might think. You see, no other

---

* Note, by the way, that we speak of ourselves with the pronoun "we," known as the majestic plural or *pluralis majestatis*. (It's Greek to many, but it's Latin, actually.)

book ever put before the human race has known that its reader exists!* No other book, except the one your eyes behold at this very moment. We were waiting for you and you alone, as you'll soon see and know without a doubt. Yes, you.

We see great potential in you—untapped powers that are ready to emerge. Just how can we know this? It's quite simple, really. Don't be alarmed, but we're *inside* your head. Perhaps a brief lesson in anatomy is in order.

As you gaze upon these letters, the flower-like *iris* of your eye blossoms to allow our symbols to *refract* through your *lens*. Our symbols then project through your mysterious *dark chamber*, on their way to your *optic nerve*. (By the way, another word for *nerve* is *mettle*, which derives from *metal*, the very stuff of alchemy.) And so our symbols, through an undeniably magical process, commingle with your gray matter (the *prima materia* of alchemy), allowing us to know one another.

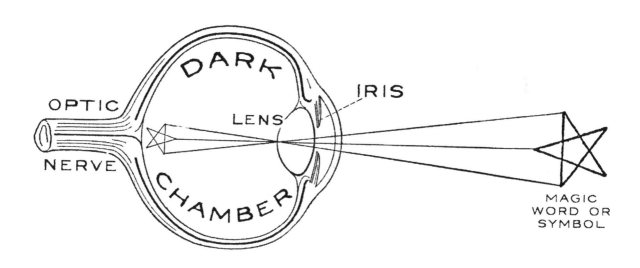

* It goes without saying that there have been magical *scrolls* that know their readers exist. We're referring, of course, to those ancient Japanese scrolls that became alive and self-aware on their one-hundredth birthday. Loose papers nothwithstanding, we are the first sentient *book*.

9

Such great potential—and yet you're full of questions and doubts. Yes, we can see the doubts brimming right up to the surface, and the questions threatening to spill over the side! You ask yourself, will a knowledge of magic words truly help me? Is magic still as vital a force as it was in olden times? (And how about that word *olden*? Is it too olden-fashioned for us to be using it? you ask.) Am I ready to begin this study, and am I ready to wield the power responsibly? Most importantly, are my intentions pure? Am I seeking mastery for the right reasons?

Our answer to every one of your questions—even the ones you haven't yet put into words—is "yes." A knowledge of magic words will benefit you in ways you've not dared to imagine. Magic is, indeed, still as vital a force as it was in olden times. Just between us, magic is *more* powerful than ever because the common people's ignorance of mystic principles puts the wizard at an even greater advantage. What *they* don't know, *you* can make the most of.

You are most certainly ready to begin this study, and the proof is that your eyes are reading these very words. (Also these.) Whether or not you'll wield your power responsibly is of course up to you, but we're an excellent judge of character, if we say so our (majestic) selves. Consider this: had we deemed you unworthy, we could have shed the ink of this text like a serpent sheds skin. ("Serpent sheds skin" is a tongue twister, as you just noticed. Say it ten times fast and it will no longer be a game, as you'll see when you thumb over to the chapter entitled Dangerous Words and Spells.)

The purity of your intentions? Well, even if you've entertained selfish desires on occasion (and we know you have . . . you know the times we mean), rest assured that magic has built-in checks and balances. We'll be so bold as to reveal a secret even now: magical acts of the greatest good can, ironically, be the most self-serving, as the energies you send out invariably come right back to you. (Like a boomerang, yes. And that goes a long way toward explaining a magic spell that will one day delight youngsters in a so-called Neighborhood of Make-Believe: *Boomerang Toomerang Soomerang.*)

As to the question of whether you seek mastery for the right reasons, here are just some of the positive qualities you possess:

* an open mind

* a healthy curiosity

* a degree of optimism

* a desire to explore the nature of reality more deeply

* a hunger for uncommon knowledge

* an unused potential

* a yearning to experiment and thereby to grow into something *more*.

These are all the right reasons, to be sure. And though you sometimes worry about your decisions and are too critical of yourself, that analytical part of your nature can also be turned to your advantage.

And so let us step together into a sparkling realm where all is fresh and unusual, yet somehow familiar and comfortable. Like your backyard after the season's first fire ceremony, a world we instinctively know shall be illuminated in a brand new way. Playfulness is crucial, if we are to follow the wisdom of the Scythian philosopher Anacharsis: "Play so that you may be serious."

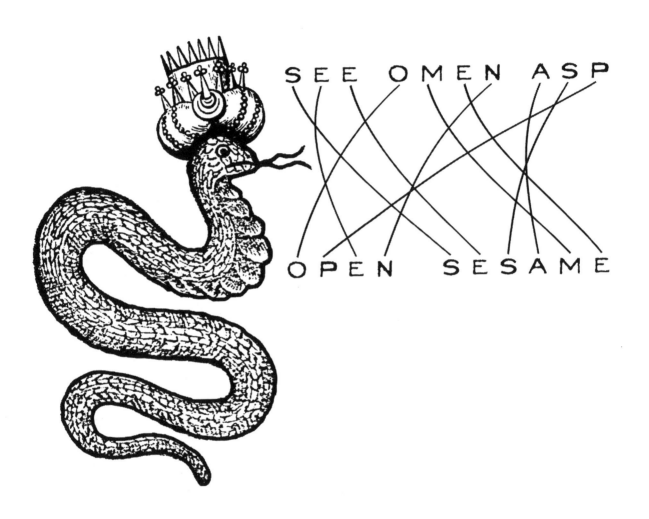

SEE OMEN ASP

OPEN SESAME

The Secrets of How to Speak Magically

You want to rise from your current magic ability to something higher. Very admirable! And you realize that success depends largely on what magic words you say and how you say them. (You have a marvelous magical accent, incidentally.) It's true that speech improvement leads to power. Unconsciously, you're mispronouncing many common magic words. No, no, it's not your fault. It's because you so often hear apprentice-wizards speak incorrectly. But the sooner we address this, the better.

One secret is to spend as much time as possible with very learned wizards who speak correctly. Oh, yes, you do already know a few learned wizards, though they may be in magical disguise. Look for someone who has a cheerful personality and small laugh lines around the eyes, telltale signs of a genuine wizard. We think you may have even been talking to one this week.

Listen carefully, focused on what you're hearing. As a rule of thumb, sit face to face and lean forward just a little to indicate that you are interested and fully alert. Be sure not to fidget or interrupt. Pay attention not only to the words but to the tone of voice. Be aware, too, of body language—what is the wizard communicating non-verbally? What do the pauses say? In your own time, imitate the wizard's speech.

Meanwhile, practice the following tips for instantaneous results.

Ten Important Rules for Speaking Magically

1. Use correct posture to help yourself think clearly and speak magic words forcefully. We can see how you're positioned right now, and there's definitely room for improvement! Sit or stand comfortably

with both feet firmly on the ground. Lift your chin slightly, pull your shoulders back, straighten your spine, and expand your chest. Be yourself, easy and natural, not stiff but dignified. There. That *does* feel better, doesn't it?

2. Breathe deeply but comfortably. Here's an experiment: Without drawing a deep breath, read aloud as much of this page as possible until you feel the need to inhale. Then take three deep breaths, holding the final breath for a few moments before exhaling. Again read aloud as much as possible of this same page. You'll immediately see that your lungs provide the power by which magical speech is produced. When your lungs are properly expanded, your chest acts as a sounding board and produces magical resonance. Practice deep breathing throughout the day, filling your lungs from the bottom to the top.

3. Open your mouth fully so as to prevent *nasality*, which is a "through the nose" speaking effect. (Yes, exactly like the way *he* talks. We didn't want to mention any names, but you're thinking of the person we had in mind.) In fact, picture a great, round crystal ball when you speak. Envision it so clearly that you can see it floating before you.

   To warm up your mouth so as to avoid nasality, say the following in as full, round tones as possible, over and over again: "Oh, my round, round ball, full of foretoken omen." Yes, you can stop now, though we do encourage you to resume the exercise later. But let's move on to the next point.

4. Develop a natural and easy style of talking, keeping your voice loud enough to carry the magic spell but no louder. Never waste force in speaking at a higher volume than necessary. The wizard who shouts is less impressive than the wizard whose voice holds its power in reserve. In fact, this principle is one of the great secrets of wizardry: *Always hold part of your energy in reserve, so that you can harness it when needed.*

5. Speak slowly so as to avoid slurring your magic words. If quick speech runs two separate magic

words together, they form a compound word that may have a different meaning—and different consequences!

6. Study your dictionary of magic words carefully so as to gain self-confidence. Constantly enlarge your vocabulary. Learn the meaning of each new magic word you meet.

   Turn to any page of a large magical tome, and you will find a great many magic words you don't know. Don't be discouraged—every magic word that enters your vocabulary is an added power. Resolve to allow no magic word to pass you without possessing its secrets.

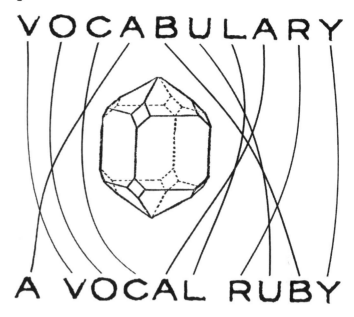

VOCABULARY

A VOCAL RUBY

7. For better enunciation, practice speaking words in a loud, clear *whisper*. This is a very subtle and little-known secret that works wonders.

ENUNCIATION

INCITE A NOUN

8. Make your speech musical, clear, and rich in tone. As a start, experiment with reading your magic texts aloud and giving more meaning to

important words by slightly changing the tones of your speech. This will improve your tonal flexibility, and you'll achieve musicality through rising and falling pitch. Oh, no, a harp will not be necessary.

9. Take a moment to think clearly before you speak a magic spell. Know what you are going to say, and only then say it and *mean* it.

10. Allow your face to light up as you intone your magic words. The challenge is to shed your masks and reveal your true wizardly personality. A radiant countenance doubles the effectiveness of magic words. Sunscreen? No, you won't need it, assuming you're practicing this exercise indoors.

Here is one of the most protected secrets of magic: a wizard can transform *any* word into a powered projection. That's because the very act of speech is the ancient "open sesame" of wizardry. The true power of the magic word lies in the mind of the wizard.

And here's the first step toward transforming any word: gaze upon it until it begins to look weird. The moment you give close attention to a word (or even a semicolon) it becomes mystifying. "Weird" commonly refers to strangeness, but remember its original meaning: *having the power to control destiny.* Give it a try—stare at a word.

In fact, why not stare at the word "word"? After all, the word *word* has a long history of unlocking enchanted realms, summoning spirits, holding demons at bay, and sanctifying spaces. A great poet will one day exclaim that nothing in the world has as much power as a word, and that we can write a word and look at it until it begins to shine. So stare at the word *word* until it shines with such weirdness that you're certain the spelling must be incorrect.

With practice, you can make any word weirdly your own, so that its deepest, most mysterious power flows comfortably and seamlessly from your lips. To tap into a word's supernatural forces, you must first know its weirdness.

Here's another word to practice with, the very word at the heart of both our magical grammar and our magical glamour: *grimoire*. Stare at it until it looks otherworldly and supernatural, like something a ghost might have written. Stare at it until it reveals itself to be an eldritch container of ancient mysteries. Allow the letters to become hieroglyphs. Notice now how they seem to make time itself luminous.

Soon magical speaking will be second nature to you. Then it will be time to sample some advanced techniques for refining and further empowering your verbal transformations. You'll find these below. No, you don't need us to tell you: you'll know when you're ready.

Eight Ways to Speak More Magically

1. Vibrate. The secret is to vocalize as much vibration as possible, as if you were a grimalkin* purring the repeated spell of a mantra. Allow the vibration to spread from your vocal cords into your entire chest cavity. This enables the magic to emanate.

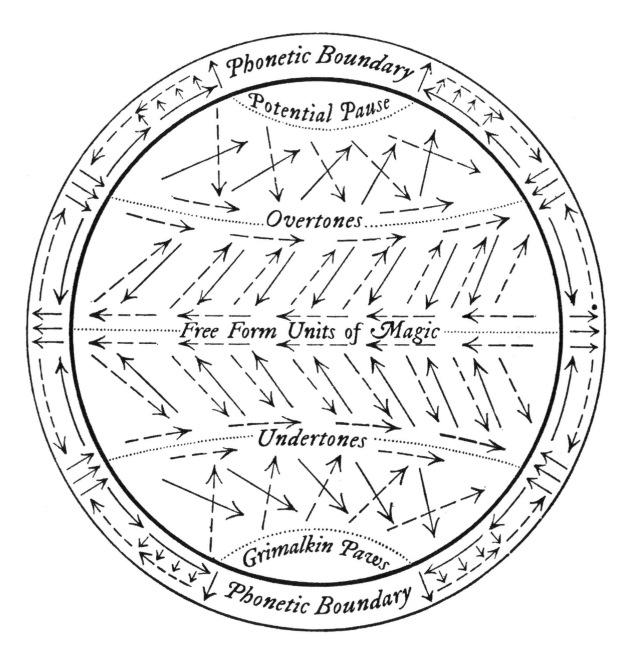

---

* No problem; we'll wait while you look it up—we need to dust the second-story page numbers.

2. Elongate vowels. That's a sure way to engender a dreamy, otherworldly quality to a word of enchantment. If you elongate your vowel sounds enough, you'll find yourself singing. Singing magic words is quite natural, as they have traditionally been sung. Indeed, the Germanic word for magic formulae is *galdr*, derived from the verb *galen*, "to sing."

3. Savor syllables. Delight in the magic word as you speak or sing it, as you might savor a morsel of fine chocolate. Intone the word as if you can taste it. Take, for instance, *hocus pocus*, with its soft and hard sounds (from the long *O* to the short *K*) like the nuts and nougat in a piece of candy. Note that the phrase has silences between syllables and between words, like pauses in our chewing.

   Hocus pocus comes into being on the whirling eddies of your breath, with the hard *hhh* sound clearing a path for the *cuss* sound. The phrase is then propelled by the plosive *P* of *pocus*, blown like a kiss to a distant grandmother. Then the softly hissing *sss* trails off into the unknown. Remember that you can literally breathe life into words! Like sylphs, words are spirits of the air.

4. Embrace the power of softness. Practice saying a magic word softly, as if it were a dim, distant memory, as if you were conjuring it from your own depths, where it had been locked away for safekeeping. Speak a magic

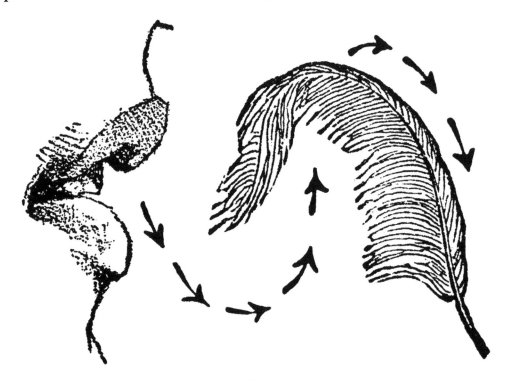

word as if you might never utter it again, with all the innocent awe of a small child appealing to a parent. If you think about it, a baby's first words are always magic incantations, sounds uttered to conjure its mama. In addition to embodying magical expectations, a baby's incantations are characterized by surprise and excitement, two crucial qualities for magic words.

One easy way to test the softness of your magical speech is to hold a feather near your lips. Attempt to leave the feather unruffled by your voice.

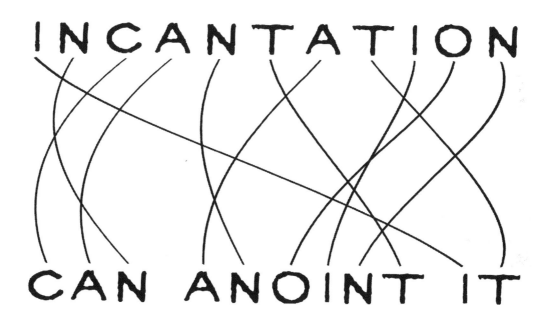

INCANTATION CAN ANOINT IT

5. Respect consequences. Speak your words of magic with all the weight of saying "I love you" to someone for the very first time. A magic word spoken with a vivid awareness of consequences will sound adventurous but not reckless, courageous but not haughty, determined but not pushy. In giving voice to the magic word, you will show the perfect balance of control and uncertainty, pairing your confidence with the tense energy of mystery. When a magic word is imbued with this quality of wonder, some people might rightly describe it as sounding "spooky" or supernatural. (Yes, we magic books get shivers up *our* spines, too.)

6. Find the word's *dimensionality*—its shape and weight. Imagine the word hanging in the air, then find its edges. Speak the word as if you were presenting a lost relic from another time. As a wise man will note, just

as the sounds made by various birds, such as crows, are carried to various distances according to the air-dividing *shape* of each particular cry, so it is with human language.

Our illustration depicts a shape for *Shirac* (pronounced *sure-rack*), the Armenian magic word for creating illumination

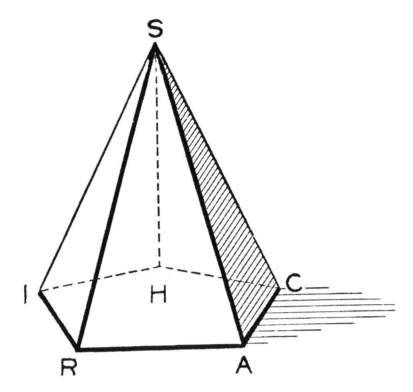

at the tip of your magic wand or staff. This is merely one of any number of shapes you can imagine for a magic word.

Here's another example, for the Egyptian word *Heka*. Pronounced *heck-ah*, the word conjures the primordial thread of magic that connects and interpenetrates all things. The original hieroglyph of the word showed a lamp-wick and an outstretched arm, symbolizing fire from a wizard's hands.

Similarly, here's the Zimbabwean magic word *Zengawii*, for restoring the pieces of a broken object. We foresee that the word will be popularized by a scribe whose Ashkenazic name means "someone who lives on a corner of land."

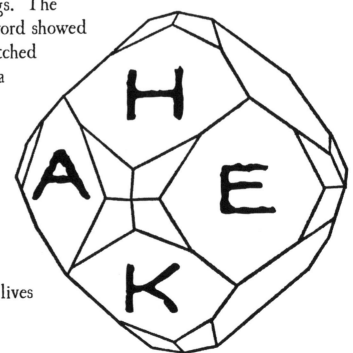

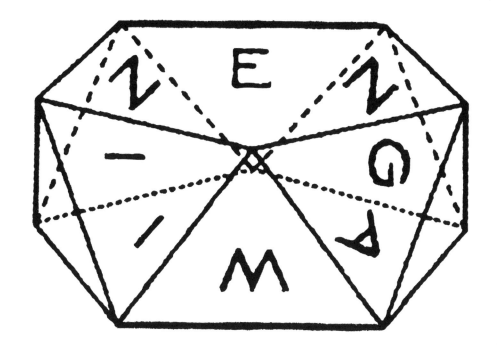

Through these examples, we have revealed a great and long-protected secret of wizardry: anything that we crystalize has a greater power.

Alternately, you may envision your word as a line in space rather than as a shape. For example, here is Xatanitos stretching forward. (Don't be put off—we know what you're thinking, and let us assure you that this word has nothing to do with the red fellow with the pointy horns.) We find this word of good luck in the Egyptian book of magical talismans* entitled Treasure of the Old Man of the Pyramids. Intoning Xatanitos is especially recommended during games of chance or skill.

---

* The root of *talisman* is the Greek *telos*, which refers to design, purpose, intent, and result.

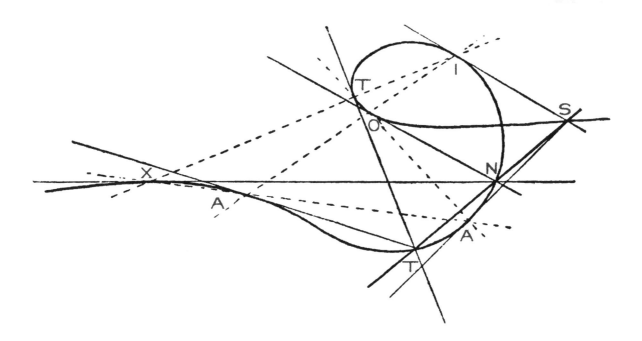

As you contemplate a word in geometric space, consider this: the letters of MAGIC SPELL recombine into CALLS PI GEM. *Pi*, of course, is the Greek word for antiquity's most mysterious number, mystically bridging the linear and curved worlds (diameter and circumference). The digits of Pi are without end, just as the energy of the universe is infinite.

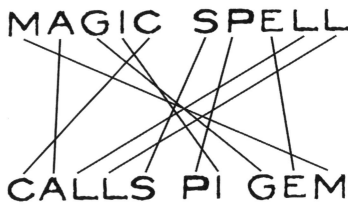

7. Cultivate reverence. To acquire that age-old respect for wizardry, speak magic words carefully, artfully, and with high esteem. Proper reverence is essential for enchantment to occur.

8. Speak the magic word from your heart. And if, when the magic moment arrives, no sound escapes your lips, then let silence be louder than words. Sometimes transcendent experiences are just too magical for words.

How to Automatically Speak Magic Words

Automatically? You're wondering what exactly we mean by that. Are we proposing you adopt some kind of goofy mechanical voice?

In fact, intoning magic words in the manner known as *automatic* has nothing to do with gadgets. Instead, it's a technique for when the hubbub of one's conscious mind makes it difficult to focus on the right magic word for a particular situation. In such cases, it's both possible and preferable to intone your magic words automatically.

To prepare for automatic speech, all that is required is some relaxed breathing and a silent statement of intention. Decide that you *will* speak the ancient language of magic. Assume the wizard's five-pointed star stance: Stand with your legs somewhat more than shoulder width apart. Hold your head upright. Stretch your arms straight out to the sides. Turn your left hand palm up and your right hand palm down. You almost have it . . . try to keep your head from tilting to one side, though. There, that's perfect!

Holding this position, quiet your mind for several moments. From that silence, syllables will begin to arise. Open your mouth and allow those syllables to emerge.

Here are the steps in a nutshell for when you come back to this page (and you shall! We'll be glad to see you here again).

1. Breathe for relaxation.

2. Silently decide that you *will*.

3. Assume the wizard's five-pointed star stance.

4. Quiet your mind.

5. Open your mouth to allow sounds to come forth.

If your tongue seems to need loosening up, intone *ab-a-ra-ca-da-ba-ra* and then allow other syllables to come to light. If the sounds seem like gibberish, that's only because they contain more meaning than you can readily interpret. You may wish to have a fellow wizard write it all down.

If your first try at automatic speech isn't fruitful, here are some troubleshooting tips to get you on the right track:

1. Lift your tongue ever-so-slightly. If your tongue is resting in the bed of your mouth, it may fall asleep completely. Lifting it a bit will put it into "ready" mode. To understand how to hold your tongue in readiness, imagine the experience of wanting to blurt something in a conversation but not getting the chance. Your lips open slightly, your teeth part, and your tongue hovers as it waits for the right moment.

2. Are you unconsciously holding your breath? Sometimes when we're nervous, we forget to breathe deeply and perhaps even stop breathing for a time. Regular, relaxed breathing is crucial for automatic speech.

3. Maybe your mind is racing. If you catch yourself on a train of thought, simply notice that you are thinking and return to a quiet state of mind. A clear head is absolutely required for automatic speech.

How to Teach a Raven to Speak Magic Words

Yes, ravens are mighty clever and very magical, but you still have to teach them. Luckily, you're perfectly qualified for this job!

1. To start on the right footing, invite the raven to perch upon your magic wand or staff. Such a gesture of trust and respect can make all the difference.

2. Remove shiny amulets and magic mirrors, lest they prove distracting. (They do have a way of collecting, don't they!)

3. Make sure your raven classroom is free of non-educational noise during the training sessions.

4. Begin with a single-word spell.

5. Look the raven in the eye and speak clearly and spiritedly so as to catch and hold the bird's interest. Repeat the word until the sand runs out of an hourglass that is half full. (If you're pressed for time, use an hourglass that's half empty.)

6. Younger ravens are more likely to want to mimic a wizard's speech.

7. Keep to a routine, scheduling your training sessions at the same time each day.

8. If the bird seems to lack respect, be sure to wear your best pointed hat. Note that your *best* pointed hat will not necessarily be your *pointiest* hat.

9. Reward the raven with praise and bits of magic apple. When the bird repeats your words with flair, offer enchanted seeds.

Some ravens never learn to speak magic words but nonetheless make useful familiars or at the very least friendly companions and trustworthy confidants.

The Secrets of How to Write Magically

If you think about it, all writing is magical. What a wizardly feat it is to hold the interest of a reader! To bring a subject to life, an author must conjure something enchanting. Through written words, a reader can live countless lives in different places and at different paces. A single sentence can span both centuries and galaxies.

The writing of magic words and spells requires the same craft as all writing. But it requires the addition of embellishments, rituals, and special touches which will lend force.

Finding the Right Brush for Spellcraft

When we paint magic words with a brush, the parchment both contains the enchantment and acts as a springboard to help the spell act more quickly. The word *ink* comes from the Greek root meaning "to burn in." A spoken magic word is a verbal contract, but the use of ink makes it a written contract.

The proper brush allows a wizard to paint an infinity of magic configurations. A wizard needs a brush that can respond quickly and reliably to subtle magical commands. Though a quill pen is handsome and serviceable for spellcraft, its hollow shaft

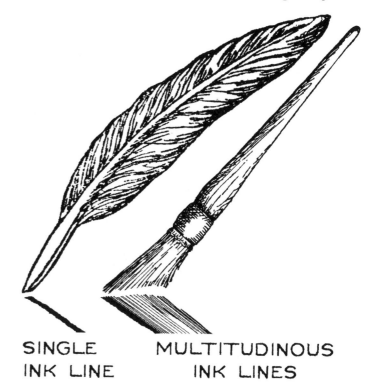

SINGLE INK LINE   MULTITUDINOUS INK LINES

paints just a single line of ink. However, the hundreds of animal hairs in a brush paint hundreds of spells at once. One talisman painted with a brush is equivalent to the power of a thick bundle of talismans.

The two main types of brushes for spellcraft are goat's hair and wolf's hair.

Goat's hair brushes are white, soft, very absorbent, and bend gracefully for fancy brushwork. Such brushes are recommended for painting the most ancient magic scripts and for any spell that calls for delicacy.

GOAT'S HAIR
SPELLCRAFT
BRUSH

The wolf's hair brush may be black, white, or brown. Its bristles are stiff and resilient, leaving sharper lines. This is a good brush for painting airy spells that benefit from the bristles splitting and leaving white spaces within the strokes.

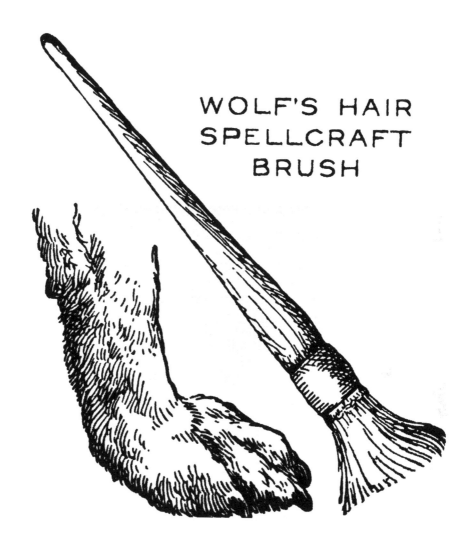

WOLF'S HAIR
SPELLCRAFT
BRUSH

A wizard's spellcraft brush should be cleaned only in the waters of a spring-fed babbling brook, of course. In wintertime, a gingerly melted icicle will suffice. Brushes are always stored with the bristles pointing up, to protect them from being crushed by the weight of the handle.

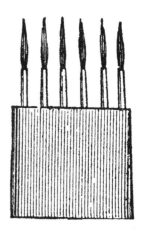

When a brush wears out and it comes time to procure a new one, some wizards bury them and some burn them. However, we strongly recommend laying retired brushes to rest in an ornate chest to honor the magic they have helped you to bestow. Try it and see for yourself that it feels proper.

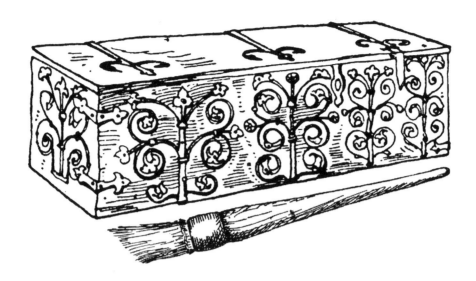

A Bridge to the Direct Experience of Magic

We write magic words so as to transmit them through time and space. And we inscribe talismans with shapes and signs because the symbol is the bridge between the ordinary world and the direct experience of magic. For all its simplicity, the circle is crucial to magic. It is the circle, after all, that transforms the mystic pentagram into a talismanic pentacle ready for magic.

PENTAGRAM   PENTACLE

The sphere of magic is a circle of which the center is everywhere and the circumference is nowhere (the *Hermetic axiom*). Here's something to ponder: all beings in the cosmos circle endlessly around a center and are themselves center-points for other beings.

Magic Mirrors of Ink

As you practice drawing perfect circles, go ahead and fill one with ink to create something marvelous. While painting magic words onto a talisman, a magician of old spilled a puddle of ink and was astonished. Reflecting and absorbing light at one and the same time, his inkblot was a magic mirror. To this day, Egyptian magicians use mirrors of ink to open their eyes in a supernatural manner, to make their sight pierce into the invisible world.

Though any wizard can use a magic mirror of ink, apprentices aged ten or younger tend to experience the most vivid visions. Magic mirrors of ink are typically poured onto parchment, but any sort of pen will suffice as long as your circle is completely filled. The mirror is empowered by beseeching two genii (resident spirits) whose names are Tarshun and Taryooshun.

In the magic mirror pictured, you'll see that the circle of ink is placed in the middle of a magic square. The figures it contains are Arabic numerals (4, 9, and 2 in the top row; 3, 5, and 7 in the middle row; and 8, 1, and 6 in the bottom row), with the horizontal, vertical, and diagonal rows all adding to fifteen.

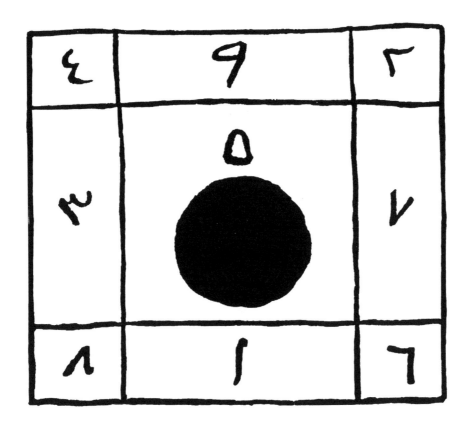

Why do all the rows add to fifteen? Many people who are supposed to become great magicians have something very important that happens to them at age 15—a life-changing event. When it happens, you know it. Additionally, fifteen is favored for divination because it is associated in the occult traditions with fate, mystery, and talismanic work. Fifteen is also associated with Saturn, the sixth planet from the sun (and in numerology, the digits of 15 are added to make 6). Saturn is the planet of time, and so the Hermetic name for this number grid is "the square of Saturn." (Drawing an unbroken line connecting the numbers in order from one to nine will form the Sigil of Saturn, the symbol of the magical essence of the planet. This symbol is used ritually to unlock the secrets of chronological time.)

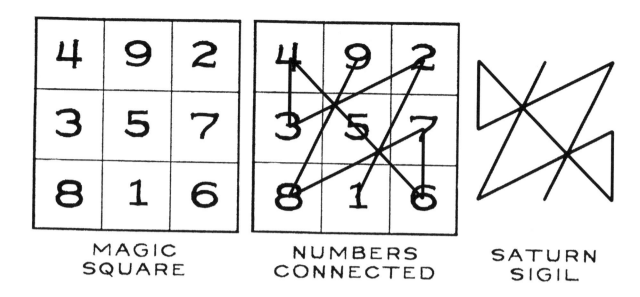

MAGIC
SQUARE

NUMBERS
CONNECTED

SATURN
SIGIL

The ancient Taoist alchemists used this magic square to conjure the harmony of the cosmos, as the grid is a map of the balanced flow of natural and supernatural energies. Notice how odd and even numbers alternate around the square's edges (the even 4 is bordered by the odd 9, followed by 2, 7, 6, 1, 8, 3); the four even numbers (4, 2, 8, 6) are at the four corners; the five odd numbers form a cross in the center of the grid (the vertical 9, 5, and 1 intersected horizontally by 3 and 7); every number pair bounding the central 5 (i.e., 4 and 6, 3 and 7, 8 and 2, 9 and 1) adds to 10. To those occultists who consider 15 the number of the Devil, we simply refer to the magic square and ask what in heaven or earth is diabolical about such perfect balance.

The circular mirror of ink is well-placed in the 5 square, for several reasons. The Pythagoreans considered the number 5 to be circular, as it produces itself in its last digit when raised to its own power (5 x 5 = 25). In ancient Greece and Egypt, the number 5 was used talismanically to keep out evil spirits, so a magic mirror of ink in the 5 square is protected from wicked influences. As the cosmos is made up of the five elements of water, earth, air, fire, and ether, a magic mirror in the 5 square spans the breadth of all existence. Ultimately, the number 5 suggests the pentagon, which engenders infinite repeatability and thereby creates a harmonious feeling. Note how each pentagon contains a pentagram, and how each pentagram surrounds its own smaller pentagon. The process continues infinitely.

Little wonder that the number five has been considered an emblem of perfection through recorded history around the world.

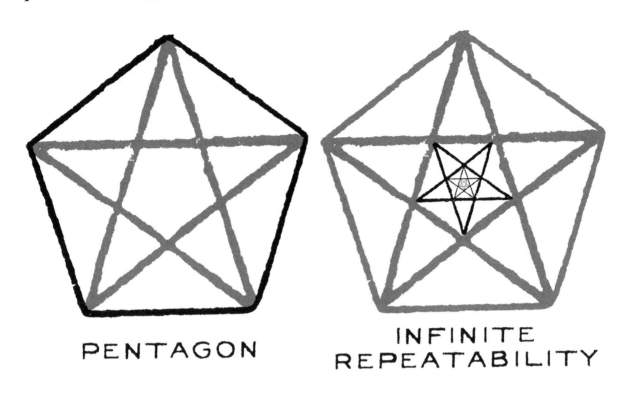

PENTAGON

INFINITE
REPEATABILITY

Magic Word Sigils

Where would wizards be without circles? (Why, they'd be running around in . . . ovals, we suppose.) We practice drawing our circles because they are the containers for our sigils—magic words in symbolic form. And we craft these glyphic seals by combining the letters of a magic word into a single abstract picture. We do this to allow the word to be stranger and more mysterious. This increases our own wonderment and makes for better magic.

We also form sigils to allow the magic to go *beyond* our native tongue. This veils the truth from non-wizards yet enables the wise to understand it throughout time in the universal language of symbolism.

As you fashion a sigil, you may leave out the vowels, if you wish. (We happen to love vowels, but to each one's own.) You may also leave out repeated consonants, at your discretion. Otherwise, follow your intuition and try out different arrangements until you are pleased with the overall visual impression. A great visionary will one day proclaim that the true method of knowledge is experiment.

In this first example, see if you can fathom what magic word has been transformed into a sigil.

Exactly! We fused together the letters of *Pocus.* In our sigil, the *S* flows into the *C*, which flows into the *U*, like the winding body of a rattlesnake. At the head of the serpent is the *P*, and at the tail, the *O* like a rattle. Without *Pocus,* of course, there could be no *Hocus Pocus.* The calling of names is a magical action surpassing all others.

In our next example, we combine the letters of Sim Sala Bim, that great all-purpose magic spell that echoes* from the troll-infested fjords of

---

* As a great Welsh chronicler of Merlin will one day reveal, if you find a dying echo and promise to build an altar for it when it falls silent, you can persuade it to tell you extraordinary things.

Scandinavia to the genie mirages of Turkey's Karapinar desert. We began with the serpentine S at the center, then intuitively added the M, like horns or ears. The I rises like an antenna, balancing the B on its spine. The L dangles from the S, further supporting an A and its mirror image.

Those *A*'s recall the grandest yet simplest axiom of Hermes, the messenger of the gods and patron of mages: "As above, so below." This is the secret key to understanding all mystic lore, and with this knowledge alone you may work miracles. The axiom means, "as in the spiritual, so in the material world." Think about how, by looking into a pool of water and studying a reflection, you can learn something about the object above that casts that reflection.

The atoms of our physical lives are governed by the same blueprints that regulate the stars. In material nature we have a physical sun that distributes light and warmth. In the spiritual world we have an invisible sun that enlightens the heart and spreads the warmth of love as it illuminates life's mysteries. A corollary to the axiom is, "As within, so without." That means that each of us is the entire universe in miniature form. As a great allegorist will proclaim, the human house is a paradox, for it is larger inside than out. In other words, a single person's awareness is woven into the nature of everything. This is why the most efficient way to transform the world is to change oneself. Another way to phrase the axiom is, "From one, know all"—the greatest secret of mind reading!

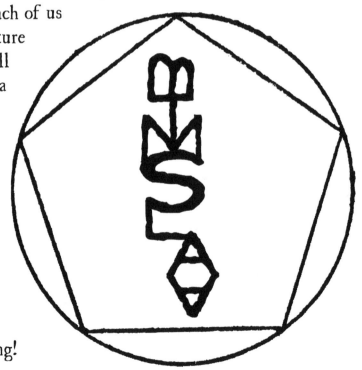

The following sigil incorporates the discrete letters of the magic word *Ablanathanalba* (pronounced *ab-la-nath-a-nal-ba*), the name of the supernatural guardian of an ancient Egyptian shrine—a griffin (also spelled *gryphon*) with a lion's body, mane, and legs, and an eagle's head, face, wings, and talons. Yes, such a creature *is* a little difficult to visualize, so we've included a picture. It looks familiar, doesn't it? You've seen griffins before, though until now you've never been formally introduced.

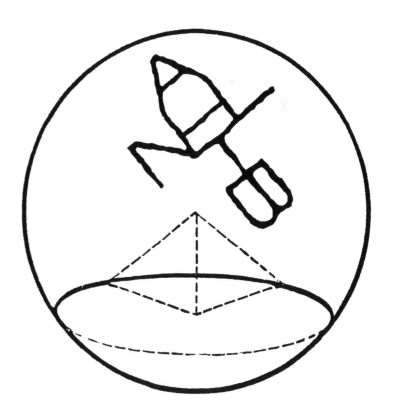

In Greek, the name of this griffin reads the same backward as forward. The name is a charm to protect against the forces of ill will, and it can be painted on the back of a statue or any other object requiring safeguarding. But the name also opens up a cosmic space of light in which the griffin can appear and give oracular advice. For that purpose, the full spell is: "May there be depth, breadth, length, brightness, *Ablanathanalba*."

Our next sigil is for *Jingo*, the name of a legendary Empress who ruled Japan and was recognized as a goddess a century later. She is said to have possessed a pair of divine jewels that allowed her to control the rising and falling of the sea. Just as the expression "by Jingo" is a euphemism for the deity, "high Jingo" refers to exalted magic. We incorporated a crescent moon into the *0*, by Jingo!

The moon is another controller of tides, and the crescent is one of the oldest symbols known. In ancient Babylonia, the crescent represented the moon as "the lamp of Heaven and Earth." Our crescent here doubly suggests an eye, so as to conjure omniscience.

When space on a parchment or amulet is limited, the most concise sigil contains every letter of the alphabet as well as every number, in a single primal egg-shape. No, really, it does! *Egg* is from an Old Norse word meaning to incite action and enable a new reality. The mystical Philosopher's Egg is the substance that transmutes ordinary metals into gold. And so this egg-shaped sigil of all that can be numbered or named is powerful, indeed. Tracing out every letter and number on the sigil is an excellent way to recharge your magic wand.

The Celestial Alphabet

Another quite excellent way to grant magic words more occult power is to transcribe them in the celestial alphabet revealed by the great Welsh alchemist and mage John Dee. Dee asserts that the immortal patriarch Enoch—who the Book of Genesis says ascended to the heavens without dying—was the last human on earth to know this mysterious language. Writing magic words in the celestial script combines the power of symbolism with traditional alphabetic expression. The script is to be written from right to left. Yes, like Hebrew! Here is a chart of the characters, with their English equivalents. Note that *W* would be spelled with two *V*s.

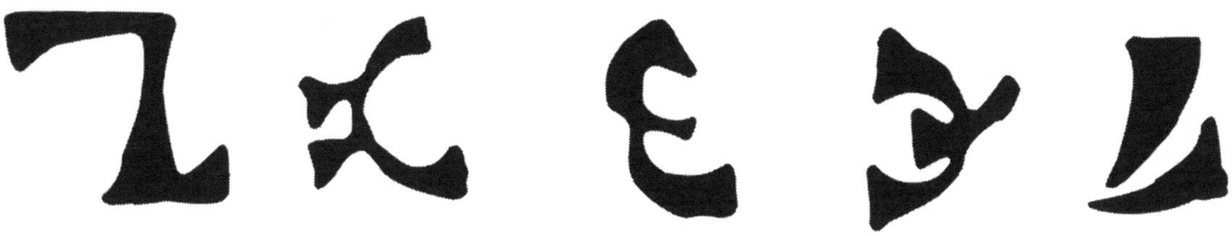

I L M N O

P Q R S T

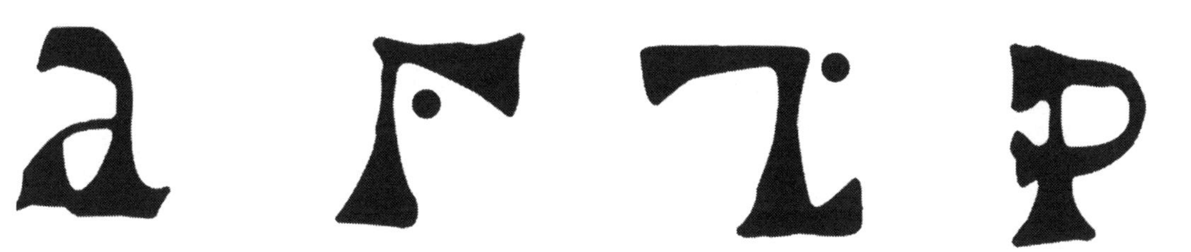

U/V X Y Z

Here's an example of a magic word transcribed into celestial script. *Anazapta* is a talisman guaranteeing longevity. Pronounced *an-a-zap-ta*, it dates to the reign of pharaoh Horemheb. The word is useful not only for immortality but for any pleasant situation or experience you wish to prolong. Summer vacation? Why, yes, that would be a perfect application.

Here's another example, in which *Yaldabaoth* is transcribed into celestial script. Pronounced *yal-da-bay-oth*, it is the name of a lion-headed serpent found on many Hellenistic Egyptian amulets. The fearsome creature breathes light power into humankind.

44

The Secrets of Magical "Automatic Writing"

Earlier, we unveiled the magical strategy of automatic speaking. Well, automatic *writing* is writing performed without conscious thought.

The wizard's hand holds a quill pen over a parchment and begins to make scrawling marks. The marks slowly begin to shape letters or symbols. Finally, entire sentences or sigils take form. This is an excellent technique for finding the right magic word when it otherwise won't pop into your head.

The most effective way to write magic words automatically is to sit comfortably in a semi-darkened room and hold your arm clear of your writing desk. Do not rest your wrist or elbows or any part of your arm on the desk. Allow your quill to lightly touch the parchment. Some wizards prefer to hold the quill between the first and second fingers; see what feels right for you. After several moments, the muscles of your hand and arm will begin to twitch, and automatic writing will begin.

As the quill begins to move, it is crucial that you disconnect your conscious mind from your hand. Turn your head away from the parchment and close your eyes. A trance state is not required; merely make your mind as blank as possible. Leave your hand to itself, even if it appears at first to write nonsense. (You may wish to keep the nonsense for your nonsense file.)

If the script is not decipherable, don't be discouraged. The cryptic writing is probably in a forgotten alphabet or a magical language! It is also possible that your magic words will come through reversed, so hold your parchment to a mirror after you complete the session.

If the magic words you write are unpronounceable, they will better serve you for talismanic use. Abstract symbols or pictograms will of course be new sigils for you to use.

With practice, you will be able to perform automatic writing while you carry on a conversation with another wizard or read a magical tome—or even while you eat a magical snack. Beginners, however, will enjoy the best results while sitting quietly alone with a blank mind. Fifteen to twenty minutes is the optimal daily sitting. As with all magical work, patience will offer rewards.

How does automatic writing provide the right magic word when the wizard doesn't consciously know it? The process allows the wizard's deepest intuition to communicate itself, unhindered by preconceptions, doubts, or distractions. Some call it the higher self or the wellspring of innate wisdom. It's the part of yourself directly connected to the source of magic. It's your innermost, portable library of everything you have read and learned since you were born. In a way, we are all "walking encyclopedias."

The Use of Invisible Magic Words

Wizards often experience an uncanny phenomenon: knowing more magic than they can put into magic words. The secret is to focus more on unwritten, invisible magic words so as to tap into your nonverbal intentions. Think of the magic lexicon as a rose window or skylight, and peer *through* the transparent words so as to focus more clearly on what you seek to manifest.

To put this technique into practice, use a quill with no ink or a paint brush with no paint and invisibly write on parchment. Unable to see the magic you are writing, you will spontaneously concentrate on and pinpoint your objectives.

Some wizards like to practice invisible writing by painting with a brush dipped in dewdrops or waved through a swirl of mist. These methods are perfectly fine, and it goes without saying that dewdrops and misty swirls from *enchanted* meadows are best, especially when the meadows are bathed in moonlight. (It's no coincidence that SUPERNATURAL rearranges into LUNAR PASTURE.) The most important thing is for your magic words to remain unreadable and therefore more intensely focused.

SUPERNATURAL

LUNAR PASTURE

There's a time-honored adage that magic words become numinous (strongly mysterious and unearthly) when the markings disappear. The true wizard can read the unwritten.

How to Write Invisible Words on Water

Wizardry alone preserves the secret of how to write invisible yet enduring magic spells on the surface of a pool of water. The surprisingly simple technique has just four requirements:

1. One shallow silver bowl
2. One horn of freshly collected dewdrops
3. One goat's hair brush
4. One sheet of blotting paper

Whereas writing on parchment with ink requires a wet brush, begin with a dry brush to write on water. Gently trace the first letter of your magic word onto the surface of the water. The bristles will absorb that letter's-worth of water. Then wipe the brush on the blotting paper to dry it again. The paper will absorb the water and the invisible letter it contains. Now trace the second letter of your magic word onto the surface of the water, and repeat the blotting process. When you finish writing on water, you will have cast your spell invisibly by virtue of the silver bowlful. Leaving traces on the water makes your spell untraceable. The unenchanted assume that writing on water is fleeting, but the blotting paper offers a lasting talisman with all the letters of your magic spell combined into an invisible sigil.

The Use of Transitory Magic Words

The art of writing magic words and symbols with a wand in the sand is called "Fu Ji" by the Taoist wizards who perfected the technique. They use a tray of sand and, by tradition, a willow wand. The reason for sand writing is simple: the shifting of the sand literally unearths the essence of magic itself. The sand embodies transitory nature. When magic words are etched into the sand, the enchantment's permanence will be inversely proportional to the sand's impermanence.

Our favorite method of ephemeral writing is to open an hourglass and write magic words on the surface of the powdered eggshells in the upper bulb. The lines of the etching will slowly disintegrate as the powder falls through the tube. This technique is obviously ideal for spells intended to take effect within an hour's time.

Deeper Secrets of Magic Brushwork

Unlike writing performed by the unenchanted, wizardly calligraphy has a life of its own. Magic calligraphy is an extension of the wizard's body and life force. The wizard's vital spark travels through the brush (like an umbilical cord) and into the "veins" of ink on the parchment. The letters and symbols that a wizard paints possess five main qualities:

SINEW

1. sinew
2. bone
3. flesh
4. energy
5. aura

BONE

If any one element is missing from the calligraphy, the spell will be less effective. All five, in delicate balance, are crucial to the magic.

The bone, of course, provides the framework on which the flesh is supported. But more than that, the bone represents the spell's firmness, its will, its dignity. Similarly, we say that a wizard who "lacks backbone" is deficient in courage or strength of character. Through the flesh that is supported by the bone, energy flows like blood through the sinews.*

FLESH

---

* Recall that destiny-controlling WEIRDNESS rearranges to RED SINEWS.

Painting too much bone and too little flesh makes for wizened magic. (Yes, it *is* curious that *wizened* has a wizardly sounding "wiz" in it. *Wizen* is rooted in words related to withering, while *wizard* is rooted in words related to wisdom.) Such calligraphy may possess the dignity of age, but it is gnarled and weak. A wizened brushstroke is often called a "broken wand." Painting too much flesh and too little bone softens the magical atmosphere (aura).

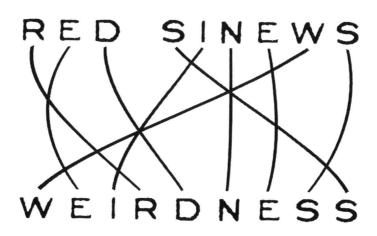

The *aura* of magic calligraphy refers to the atmosphere of elegance and charm that the brushwork exudes, like sparks from a flint. It can be likened to a person who displays charisma. It is an immaterial yet unmistakable quality. There is a magnetism—an allure—that is bewitching, entrancing, and spellbinding. Beauty is important, but beautiful writing without inner strength is like an enchanted grove whose blossoms have all fallen to the ground.

Choose carefully where you work on your calligraphy, for the mere act of practice will affect the environment! The legend is true that when calligraphy wizard Wang Xizhi sat on the bank of a pond to perfect his technique, the pond's water transformed into ink.

How to Make a Magic Ink-Stone

The writing of magic spells is best done with ink from a magic ink-stone, fashioned into any amulet shape you wish. To create one, you will need:

1. Gum arabic, 112 drachms

2. Lamp-black, 104 drachms

3. Burnt willow-wood coals, three

4. Water, one-half flagon

The best lamp-black is acquired from oil lamps used while studying magical or alchemical tomes. The brighter the light, the deeper the lamp-black.

If burnt willow-wood is not available, alder buckthorn will suffice, but be sure that the coals are collected from a ritual fire or from under a cauldron.

Pound the gum into a dust so fine it could fly away. Dissolve the dust into the half flagon of water (drawn from an enchanted well, if possible, or from the chalice of an elder wizard). Then knead the lamp-black and burnt willow coals into the gum water to make a paste. Sculpt this paste into any amulet shape you wish. (Well, we suppose you *could* use that one, but your first thought was better.) While it is still soft, make a small indentation at the top of the sculpture. When you are finished, dry your new ink-stone in a glowing furnace for four hours. After the ink-stone has cooled, brush it gently with gum water to make it jet black, shiny, and as hard as marble.

To use your ink-stone for writing magic words, put a drop of water in the indentation you made. This will dissolve into the blackest ink you've ever seen.

Here are three talismanic ink-stone shapes that might inspire you:

By the way, notice that TALISMAN rearranges into ANTI-ALMS. That is because alms are gifts of compassion for *others*, whereas a talisman is a gift to *oneself* for personal good fortune.

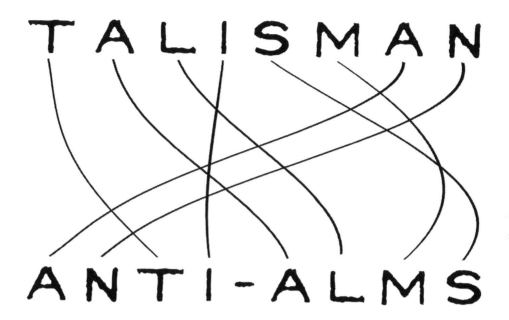

How to Frame a Far-Reaching Wish

When you have a wish that needs to cover a large area (involving a whole community, a wide region, the seven seas, the entire earth, a solar system, a galaxy, and so on), there is a simple way to give the wish a snowflake frame with an infinite circumference. An infinite circumference allows the wish the freedom to spread boundlessly.

First, write your wish at the exact center of a parchment, in small script. Second, draw a triangle to frame the wish, bringing the tips near to the edge of the parchment.

MAY THE FORESTS
SING TO THE SKIES
AND SHELTER
THE EARTH
BELOW.

Third, draw another triangle of the same size, pointing opposite the first triangle. Note that your wish is now enclosed within a hexagon flanked by six triangles. The boundary of this new shape is one-third longer than the original triangle.

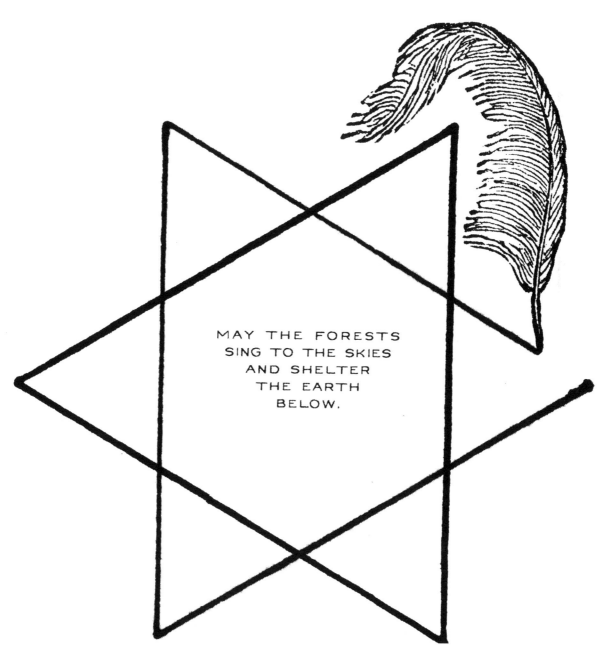

MAY THE FORESTS
SING TO THE SKIES
AND SHELTER
THE EARTH
BELOW.

Now the true magic begins, for it is time to give this shape an infinite circumference. Upon each of the six triangles, draw equal-sized but opposite-pointing triangles. This gives you eighteen triangles and, again, a circumference one-third larger.

MAY THE FORESTS
SING TO THE SKIES
AND SHELTER
THE EARTH
BELOW.

Continue the process, and notice how each time you add triangles, the snowflake's circumference lengthens even though it remains on a single page. Draw as many smaller and smaller triangles as you are able.

MAY THE FORESTS
SING TO THE SKIES
AND SHELTER
THE EARTH
BELOW.

When they are smaller than a point of ink, you will have symbolically created a frame that reaches into infinity.

MAY THE FORESTS
SING TO THE SKIES
AND SHELTER
THE EARTH
BELOW.

The secret of this magical snowflake will one day spread around the world by a wizard of numbers from an arctic kingdom.

How to Create a Magic Spell Knot

A magic spell knot is made up of graceful loops with no beginning and no end, representing limitless magic. Written into the loops are spells, traditionally for good fortune.

Start by writing down a list of short intentions or wishes. Once you have your list, carefully print the spells inside the looped knot. Start anywhere inside the knot path. Turn your parchment around as you write, following the path. The spell should flow seamlessly, with no beginning and no end. As you near the end of the path, choose a spell that will fit exactly into the remaining space. We'll provide an example on the next page.

Our example is an endless spell that will be popularized by a wordsmith who will champion self-reliant individuals. He will encourage every wizard to build one's own world according to the pure ideas in one's mind, and to allow that world to unfold its great proportions.

Allow your imagination to twist your magic spell knot into any shape. For example, here is the design of an ancient rune stone from the Scandinavian peninsula:

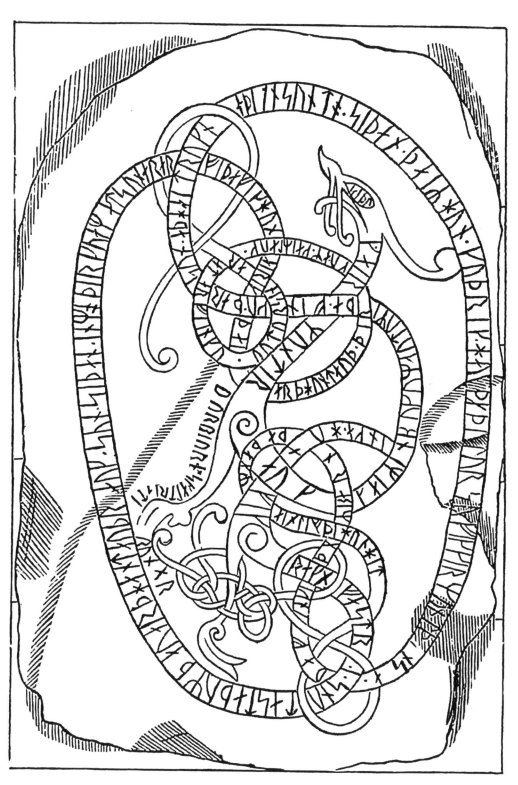

How to Use Magic Words to Give Someone the Moon

Though we detect a glimmer of doubt in your mind, it is indeed possible for a wizard of your experience to gift a friend or loved one with the very moon itself. The secret comes down to us from esoteric Japanese cosmologists known as the Onmyodo ("The Way of Yin and Yang"). The Onmyodo knew the spellbinding power of wondrous words. When one person becomes dear to another, for example, we bind that feeling with the magic word *love*. Similarly, with spellbinding words you can give someone the moon.

The spell is so astonishingly simple that the unenchanted won't even suspect that magic words are at play. The spell may be performed during any lunar phase. Point your wand directly at the moon and hold it steadily as you say these exact words: "Look in the sky at the beautiful moon. O, my esteemed one, I will give it to you. *That beautiful moon is yours.*" If your esteemed one accepts your gift, then the moon is his or hers.

One famous Onmyodo, named Abe no Seimei, was so skilled at esoteric cosmology that after his death his legend grew to Merlin-like proportions. The mystical five-pointed star (what Greek wizards dubbed the pentagram) is known in Japan as the Seal of Abe no Seimei.

Transformation Words and Spells

Ab-A-Ra-Ca-Da-Ba-Ra

This very old magic spell dates back to the Akkadian Empire and was salvaged from the extinct language of the ancient Elamites. Look carefully: the spell is not as simple as *Abracadabra*. First, note the crucial difference: two additional *A*'s:

AB RACADAB RA

ABARACADABARA

Those two *A*'s transform the five syllables of *Abracadabra* into seven, turning a single word into an entire magic chant! Whereas the syllables of *Abracadabra* form the symbol of magic itself—the pentagram, the syllables of Ab-a-ra-ca-da-ba-ra form the symbol of magical *power*—the heptagram:

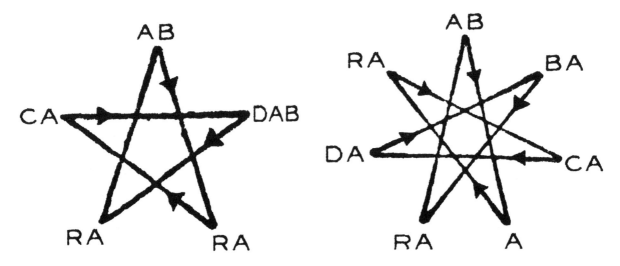

Syllables are held together by a sort of sonic glue, giving a word strength. As our diagram shows, the seven-pointed star is stronger because it's more tightly woven.

Chant the seven syllables of Ab-a-ra-ca-da-ba-ra, each of equal duration, and transformative magical energy will build. The spell's power is extraordinarily versatile, because it activates the building blocks of reality. According to your focused intention, use the spell to manifest, vanish, or levitate an object. Use it to make a wish come true, or to open a locked door. Transform any mundane situation into something extraordinary. Or diminish a negative influence by using the spell in its age-old talismanic form, reducing the letters one at a time until none remains:

ABARACADABARA
ABARACADABAR
ABARACADABA
ABARACADAB
ABARACADA
ABARACAD
ABARACA
ABARAC
ABARA
ABAR
ABA
AB
A

If you use the spell for a diminishing talisman, here is a vital secret that's rarely shared: after you print the final *A*, hold your quill over the parchment, below the *A*, and write an invisible circle in the air. Since it's about diminishment, draw the circle counterclockwise. Only this key detail will ensure a *full* diminishing influence.

Adi, Edi, Idi, Odi, Udi,
Oo-i-Oo, Idu, Ido, Idi, Ide, Ida

Can you find the magic mirror hidden within this spell? Yes, it's the *I* in the very center, which turns the first half of the spell backwards. The final word is a mirror image of the first word, the second from last word mirrors the second word, and so on. That magic mirror is central to this spell's effectiveness, as it opens a portal into the otherworld.

This spell will become famous in an emerald city as a means of transforming any foul person or thing into a pretty dove. The words require some magical passes, however. The hands must be waved, palms downward, in seven semicircles over the person or object to be transformed. To activate the spell, intone the sound *Woo* as a climax.

BENATIR CARARKA

DEDOS ETINARMI

Preserved in the grimoire *La Chouette Noire (The Black Owl)* of 1652, but tracing back to the wizards of Ancient Egypt, this spell grants invisibility and the power to penetrate any obstacle—yes, even a stone wall. *Benatir* conjures the spirit of water, and adding *Cararkau* conjures the spirit of the sea. *Dedos* conjures the spirit of earth. And *Etinarmi* conjures the spirit of air. The spell is best pronounced *Been-a-tear car-ark-ow dead-ows et-in-are-me.*

Dark, Light, Earth, Air, Sun, Truth

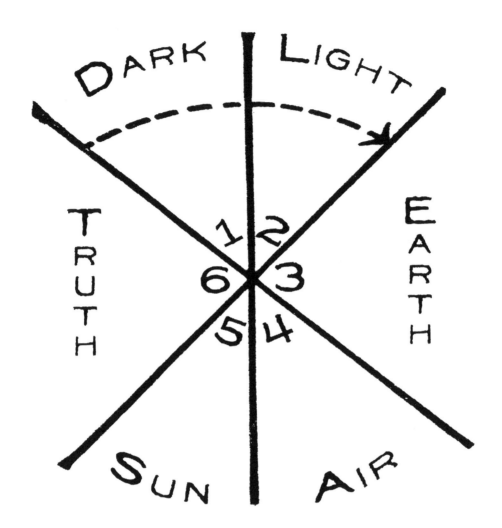

This magical incantation was explained by an esoteric Pythagorean named Androcydes. His work survives only in scattered fragments, but that is appropriate, for the smallest particles contain the whole in embryo as they're carried on the four winds across the seven seas. The spell was discovered in the temple of the huntress goddess Artemis in the ancient Greek city of Ephesus. It is used for banishing problems.

Note how each word of the spell progresses from the last and uplifts. The

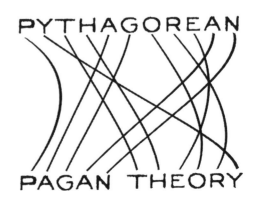

greatest transformation occurs when the first word, *dark*, is banished by the second word, *light*. When we emerge from the darkness of misfortune, we stop stumbling because we can find our footing on the *earth*. Then we can breathe again and our spirits can even soar into the *air*, where we find the sun, which illuminates the *truth*. The spell offers a six-part solution to transforming our darkest doubts into the highest certainties.

The lines of our illustration remind you of something, don't they? Indeed, the lines recall something from the Roman architect Vitruvius about the proportions of the human body as they relate to the cosmic order. Yes, the lines symbolize the wizard in the very act of transformation! And mark our words—Vitruvius will have a crater and a mountain of the moon named after him; as below, so above.

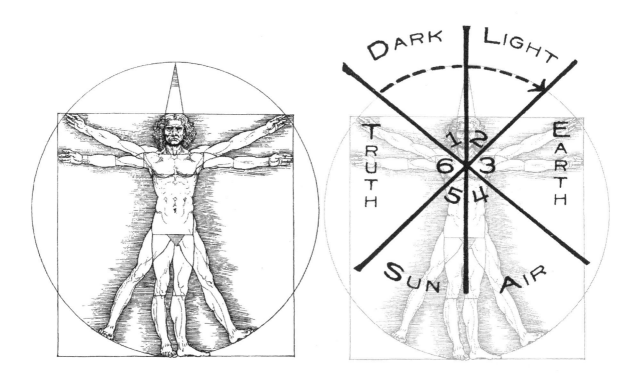

Speaking of Vitruvius, we might mention that the three "Vitrivuan Virtues" of architecture also apply to magical talismans: *firmitas* (solidity), *utilitas* (usefulness), and *venustas* (beauty).

Open Sesame

OPEN SESAME

The pods of the sesame plant burst open when their seeds reach full development. That's the mundane origin of this magic password—and we know you've wondered just where it came from! The name of the seed, from the Ancient Egyptian *sesemt*, is over 4,000 years old. The word harks back to the sound vibrations that the Chaldean priests used to open doors and levitate heavy objects.

Open sesame is the age-old key for unlocking barriers, dissolving obstacles, and revealing something beyond. It is the coveted guarded secret that grants admittance into inner chambers and secret circles. It invites us to discover long-hidden treasures and to materialize extraordinary, otherwise unattainable things. *Open sesame* guides you to find your way into the mental place where imagination resides.

Before you speak the words, you are already standing between two worlds, at a magic threshold (liminal zone), ready to call upon the veil to be parted and for a spectacle to unfold. There's already electricity in the air, sizzling with the promise of a miraculous, legendary payoff. Steeped as they are in history and romantic tales of adventure, the words *open sesame* are potent with mystery and intrigue, and they always take the

spirit back to Ali Baba's primal, womb-like cavern of wonders, that secret passage to other realms. As a pass phrase, the words may well qualify as a "worst-kept secret," but their power has not diminished. *Open sesame* is simply the thing one says when faced with an obstacle.

Pollux Castor Wasat Mebusta Alhena Tejat

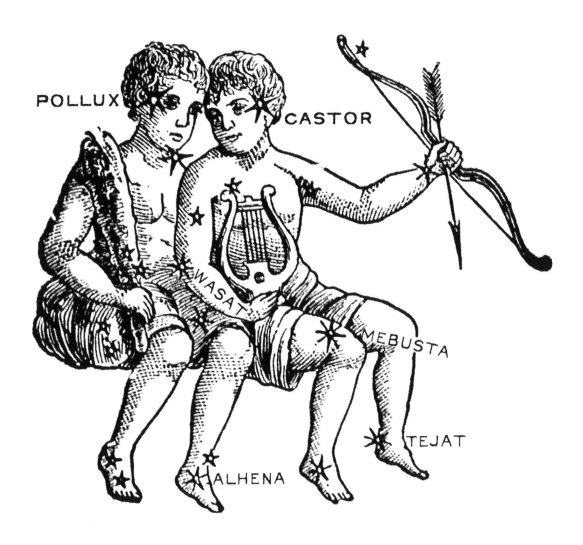

A spell for doubling anything, *Pollux Castor Wasat Mebusta Alhena Tejat* is a recitation of the major stars in the constellation of Gemini (Latin for "The Twins"). *Pollux* is a giant orange star, named after the divine son of Zeus in Greek mythology. *Castor* is actually a sextuple star system, named after the mythic twin brother of Pollux. *Wasat* is an Arabic name meaning "the Middle." *Mebusta* is an ancient Arabic name meaning "outstretched paw." *Alhena* is an Arabic name meaning "a mark (on the neck of a camel)." *Tejat* is an Arabic name whose significance has been lost.

Pyrzqxgl

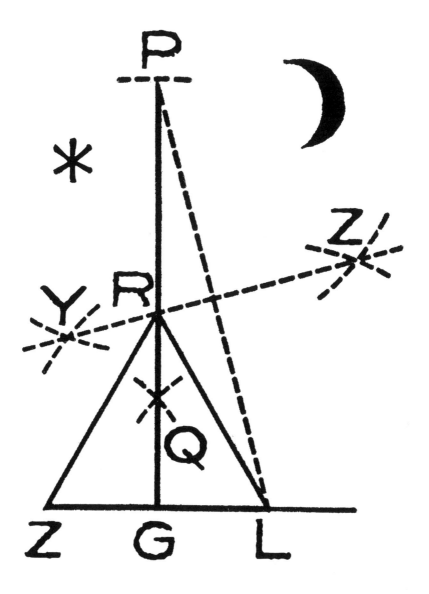

This magic word will earn renown in an emerald city as a means of transforming a person into a bird, fish, or anything else. Repeating *Pyrzqxgl* reverses the transformation. Proper pronunciation of the word is crucial to its effectiveness, and that's why it is so rarely heard—it confounds most wizards. Yet it's not quite the tongue-twister it would appear. The letters *pyrz* should be intoned like "purrs," with a strong *z* sound at the end. *Qx* is pronounced like "kicks." The final *gl* sounds like "gall." Give a very strong stress to the "kicks" in the middle to give your command a rush of power.

This Latin spell turns pussy willows back into the cats they once were. Note how the words transform as they go, with the second word changing its first two letters and the third word changing its last two letters. *Salix* is the genus of willow with downy catkins. *Felix* means happy. And *feles* is the root of *feline*. Use this spell with caution, however, as it can release more cats than one can shake a wand at.

Originating in India, the sounds of *yantru*, *mantru*, *jala*, and *tantru* evoke the Hindu words *yantra* ("instrument"), *mantra* ("formula"), *jala* ("net"), and *tantra* ("expansion"). Taken together, they form the mystical sentence, "With the proper instrument and formula, [a wizard] gains liberation through expansion."

How to Hear a New Magic Word in a Seashell

Hearing a simple ocean's roar in a seashell is all right for the unenchanted. But as a wizard you can hear much more than just an unintelligible "white noise."

It will one day be said that the ocean is a voice, that the ocean speaks to the distant stars and answers their movements in its deep and solemn language. And the ocean especially addresses itself to wizards. It speaks of the great fluid existence of life. It speaks of metamorphosis. The unenchanted hear none of this. They cannot take in the poetry of the infinite.

According to the Hermetic axiom, "as without, so within," a wizard can use a seashell to hear the voice of the ocean speaking new magic words. A seashell is a microcosm, and the mighty tides are at play in its inner sanctum*, pulled by the gravity of the full moon. Waves of sound rush from the spiral of the shell into the cochlear spiral of your inner ear. Inexplicably, seagulls are often heard as well.

Skeptics may claim that the sound one hears is the rushing of one's vital fluid. Yet a savant will one day discover that the makeup of human blood bears a haunting likeness to sea water.

And so tap a seashell with your magic wand to identify you as a wizard, then hold the shell to your ear and listen to the waves until they speak the magic you are seeking.

---

* A shell's innermost, hidden place is known in Latin as its *penetralia*.

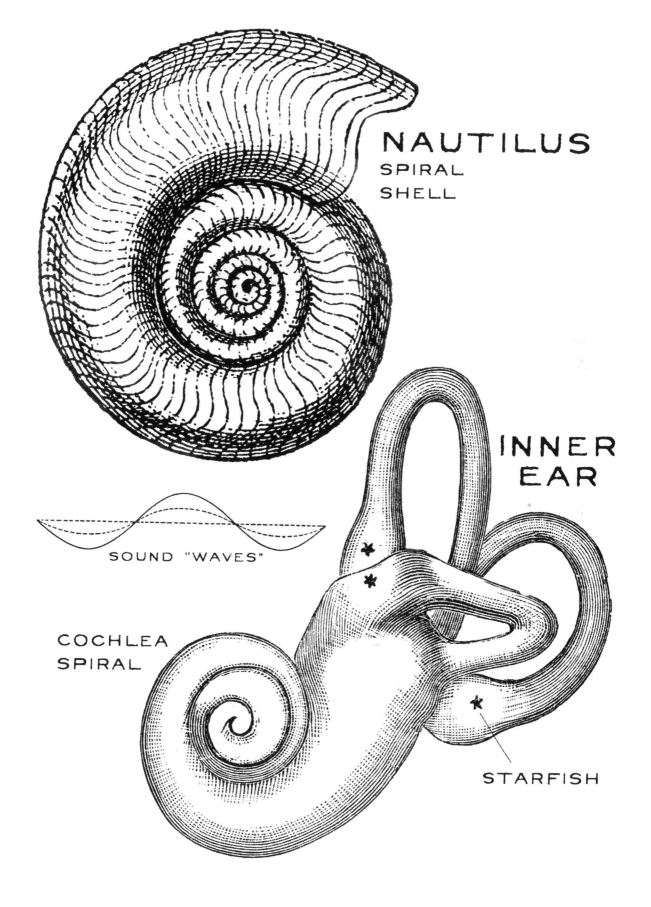

NAUTILUS
SPIRAL
SHELL

INNER
EAR

SOUND "WAVES"

COCHLEA
SPIRAL

STARFISH

The Magic Triangle that Brings Everything Together

Here is a most enjoyable experiment that will turn out magically for even the least experienced wizard. It involves a specially drawn triangle, a cauldron or bowl of water, and your pointiest wand.

The triangle you draw will have six chambers, and here is why. When we make a wish, we desire a story to unfold in a certain way. For a wish to come true, the six elements of the story must come together. The Greek philosopher Aristotle identified the six elements:

* action (the events, the process, the movement of the story)

* personae (the characters, the people involved)

* ideas (the thought at the heart of the story)

* rhythm (the throbbing heartbeat of the story, the sounds)

* language (the verbal expressions, what is communicated)

* spectacle (visual aspects)

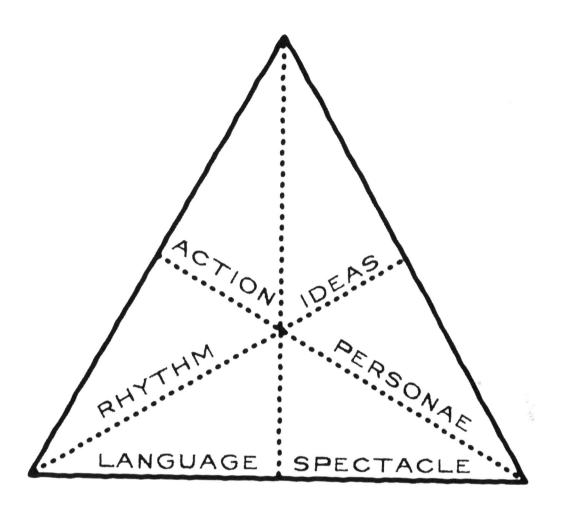

To work this magic, you will need:

1. a square of thick paper

2. a stick of graphite for drawing the triangle

3. a cauldron or bowl filled with water to float the paper upon

4. a pipette or small spoon for carefully applying drops of water into the triangle

5. a pointy wand or other sharp stick

Dip your stick of graphite in water and draw a triangle on the square of thick paper. Make dotted lines from each corner of the triangle to the middle of the line opposite, so as to mark the center of the shape.

Float the paper on the surface of the water. With a pipette or small spoon, very carefully fill the space inside the triangle with water, one drop at a time. You'll see that the droplets will remain within the dampened lines of the triangle.

Now take your pointy wand (or a needle or other thin, smooth, sharp instrument) and just barely dip its point into the triangle of water, taking pains not to touch the paper. Begin in the middle of the chamber of "action." Hold your wand steadily in place, and watch as the paper magically moves itself so that your wand rests at the very center of the triangle. Then touch your wand in the "ideas" chamber and repeat the process until all six elements of the story have come together.

Once you master this magical process, you can experiment with other sets of six words to fulfill different wishes. If you've ever seen a triangle labeled with "flour, water, eggs, butter, sugar, vanilla," you've seen a magical way to bake a cake.

Magic Word Squares

Magic squares need not be confined to numbers. One of the most famous word magic squares is an ancient charm that was discovered as graffiti in the buried city of Pompeii, after the eruption of Mount Vesuvius. The charm reads: *Sator Arepo Tenet Opera Rotas*. The phrase likely originated in Alexandria, Egypt, based upon excavated Coptic amulets, papyri, and ceramic shards. It's a palindromic charm, reading the same left to right, bottom to top, top to bottom, and backwards. It is traditionally used for putting out fires when water is unavailable, for curing fatigue during travel, and for removing jinxes. *Sator* can be defined as a maker or divine originator. *Arepo* is a name. *Tenet* means "holds" or "keeps." *Opera* refers to work or service. *Rotas* means wheels or, possibly, whirlwinds. Though the precise meaning of the sentence is deeply obscured by the mists of time, consider this possibility: "The mastermind holds the movement of the wheels [cycles of life] in his hands."

Creating Magic Word Squares

Creating your own magic word square is a highly rewarding challenge, especially if you enjoy solving puzzles. We've distilled the process into eight steps:

1. Choose a five-letter word you feel especially drawn to.

2. Write that word across the top row of a five-by-five grid.

3. Write it down the first column.

4. Write the letters in reverse order in the bottom row.

5. Write the letters in reverse order from the bottom of the right column to the top.

6. Choose a consonant you feel drawn to and write it in the center square. This will help to create a palindromic word crossing the grid vertically and horizontally.

7. Now choose one vowel and write it four times, in the squares above, below, left, and right of the center consonant.

8. This leaves four empty squares for two letters, mirrored on the diagonals.

But now that you have created an arrangement of five words, what does your magic square *mean*? Look up the words in your master wizard's library of magical tomes.

Here's a magic word square we created to help illuminate the process. You will not find such a square in any other magic tome, we assure you. We began with *Mazak*, which is the word *Kazam* as held before a magic mirror. *Kazam's* power lies in its great mystery. The word is the very definition of *secret*. It's something beyond understanding, something we can never get to the bottom of, something so wondrous it should only be whispered, if uttered at all. *Mazak* expresses something unobservable. It's a contradiction—a paradox. It's gone almost before it can be fully spoken. It's an otherworldly word that reveals the extraordinary in the ordinary.

For the magic word square's center consonant, we chose *T*, and then we surrounded it with four *E*'s. We filled in the remaining four squares with two *B*'s and two *C*'s so as to form the words *Abeca* and *Aceba*. Crossing the grid is the palindromic word *Zetez*.

```
M A Z A K
A B E C A
Z E T E Z
A C E B A
K A Z A M
```

What does our magic spell *Mazak Abeca Zetez Aceba Kazam* mean? Do the words form a sentence? *Mazak*, as we noted, is "the unobserved" or invisible. *Abeca* is from a Latin root meaning "alphabetical." *Zetez* recalls the mysterious Egyptian King Zet of the first dynasty. *Aceba* is the name of a king of Padibe (which will be called Uganda). And *Kazam*, again, refers to a great secret. So our spell beseeches two invisible (departed) African kings, one ruling at the source of the Nile (Lake Victoria in Jinja) and the other at the delta, to reveal the A-to-Z sequence of things that follow each other toward the greatest secret. The beginning and end of the Nile symbolize *Alpha* and *Omega*, the first and last letters of the Greek alphabet, which are words of power commonly included in hymns, prayers, and recitations of ceremonial magic traditions. That is because beginnings and endings, pasts and futures, intersect in the eternal present moment, at an invisible center-point around which existence revolves.

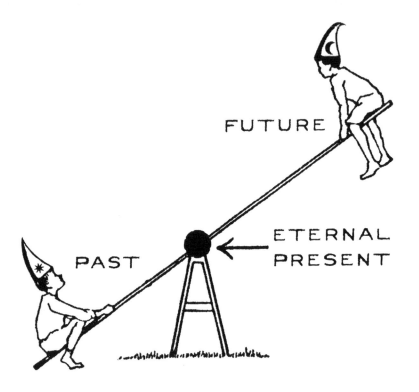

Here's another magic word square you'll find absolutely nowhere else: *Balam, Avada, Labal, Adava, Malab*:

BALAM
AVADA
LABAL
ADAVA
MALAB

Balam is the name for supernatural intuition, recalling the diviner called Balaam in the Hebrew scrolls. *Avada* is an Estonian word that means "open." *Labal* is the occult name for the revealer of all the mysteries of the Earth. *Adava* is a Marathi word for a winding road. And *Malab* is a Somali word for honey, which is a code for "alchemical gold," which itself is a code for immortality. Woven together into a grid, these magic words form a spell that conjures magic insight so as to reveal the mysterious pathway toward everlasting light.

Smaller Word Shapes

Creating magic word squares is challenging, but time and dedication will reward you greatly. We sense a question in your mind, so to be clear, wizards fashion magic word squares because the compact ordering and coherence bestows greater power. If larger word squares prove too difficult at first, try your hand at smaller shapes.

For example, here is yet another grid you will find in no other volume, this time in the shape of a wing. The words read the same both across and down.

What do the words *Hocus Omit Cip Ut S* mean, and do they form a coherent spell? *Hocus* refers to an incantation, of course. *Omit* is from the Latin meaning "let go." *Cip* is a Latin root meaning "take." *Ut,* in Medieval Latin, is the first note in the diatonic scale;

```
H O C U S
O M I T
C I P
U T
S
```

the Pythagoreans considered the first note to be the generator of the entire musical scale. *S* is naturally the serpent of alchemy. It represents the quicksilver from which springs life and renewal. It is a symbol of wisdom and knowledge uncoiling through spiritual transformation.

And so the magic spell begins to come clear. The wizard conjures the power of letting go so as to receive. This apparent contradiction is actually a great mystical secret: releasing something in order to make room for what is next, just as a serpent sheds its old skin to make room for growth. A wizard can hold more in an open hand than in a clenched fist. And so in this spell we let go to receive the first note of the musical scale, upon which harmonies can be built. The grandest symphony begins with a glyph inscribed on parchment—a single musical note.

If we reverse this same wing formation, the spell takes on a different character. *Sucoh*, of course, is *Hocus* held to a magic mirror, so as to conjure beyond dimensions. *Timo* is an Ancient Greek word meaning "I honor." *Pic* is a Romanian word for a drop of water. *Tu* means "you" in a great many languages. *S* remains the serpent, here as the age-old symbol of the life force that rises up from dark chaos into the light of a new dawn. And so *Sucoh Timo Pic Tu S* is a magical blessing of sorts, honoring the microcosm (smallest drop of water) in another person.

SUCOH
TIMO
PIC
TU
S

Crossing Word Squares

Another simpler word square to practice contains just three words, spelled horizontally, vertically, and crossing in the middle. We'll clarify this style with several examples you'll find in no other tome.

Let's begin with two related squares. The first is for bringing a dormant skeleton to life, and the second is for putting an animated skeleton to sleep. Each spell addresses *Bones*, while one conjures *Speed* and the other conjures *Sleep*. *Nomme* is a name kept on hand by spirit quellers in West Cornwall for obtaining power over ghosts.

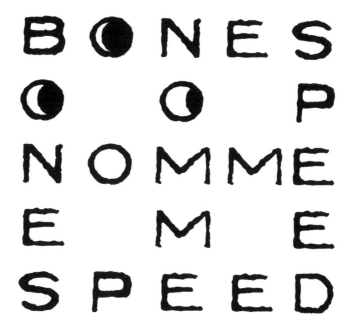

As you can see, this style of magic word square allows variation with twelve of the twenty-one letters. Once the letters in the corners, the cardinal points, and center are fixed, all the other letters may be adjusted as necessary. Looking back at our example, *Sleep* could be changed to *Steed* if a stallion would be useful, or to *Steel* if strength and firmness is required, or to *Steam* if a hot vapor is called for.

Consider our next simple square, *Accio Chosi Oriax*. The first word is Latin for "I summon." *Chosi* is a protective word of African magic that stops evil from the Otherworld. *Oriax* refers to the virtues of the stars and the mansions of the planets. So this spell is a concise way of calling upon celestial safeguarding during fearful times.

Now consider the simple square *Seven Valac Nicto*. The first word refers to the seven metals associated with the wandering stars visible to the naked eye:

```
A C C I O
C H R
C H O S I
I S A
O R I A X
```

1. Gold is ruled by the sun
2. Silver is ruled by the moon
3. Quicksilver is ruled by Mercury
4. Copper is ruled by Venus
5. Iron is ruled by Mars
6. Tin is ruled by Jupiter
7. Lead is ruled by Saturn

```
S E V E N
E A I
V A L A C
E A T
N I C T O
```

Valac refers to a revealer of hidden treasures. *Nicto* is a Latin word meaning a flash of fire. So this spell is for pinpointing secret valuables, such as shipwrecked chests of gold buried in the sand.

Note also the hidden magic word—the diamond at the center of the square, spelling *Ala* both vertically and horizontally. The sound of *ala* can represent several different meanings at once. It can mean "à la," as in the French expression meaning "according to" or "from." In this sense, *ala* communicates that a magical effect will happen *in accordance to* the proper syllables of esoteric knowledge, or that the magic

word has been handed down through the ages *from* its source. *Ala* also recalls an Arabic word that suggests an effect will occur on the authority of, or with the metaphysical assistance of, a higher power.

Here's another simple square, Sadyk Draco Kroni. The first word means "friend" and refers to the middle word, Draco, the cosmic serpent who encircles everything (also known as the tail-devouring Ouroboros of Hermeticism). Kroni is from Ayyavazhi mythology and embodies all that is sinister. So this spell handily surrounds and devours anything harmful!

The simple square *Lumos Magic Sucop* is for activating a magic mirror. *Lumos* is from the Latin word meaning "light." *Sucop* is the reflection of the magic word *Pocus,* the name of that shape-shifting Welsh spirit (*pwca*) who lives near the ancient stones and brings either good or bad fortune. This spell, written in silver ink on the back of a pane of glass, will transform it into a magic mirror for viewing past, present, or future events. The older the glass, the farther back in time it will reach.

```
L U M O S   S
U       A    U
M A G I C    C
O       I    O
S U C O P    P
```

Simple Interlocking Word Chains

An even simpler form of interlocking words is useful for channeling the swarm of ideas in your head. Begin by writing the magic word *Acba* (from the Arabic meaning "most great") across the top left of your parchment. From each letter *A,* write *Acba* down the page. Then continue intersecting the word every possible way, down and across, sometimes overlapping the letter *C,* sometimes the *B,* and sometimes the *A* again. Once you have filled the entire parchment, you will find that your mind is properly focused for spellcraft. It works like a charm because it *is* a charm.

ACBA   ACBA
C   C   C   C
B   B   B   B
A   ACBA   A   ACBA
     C   C
   ACBA   ACBA
   C A   C A
 A B   A B
ACBA   ACBA
 B   B
ACBA   ACBA
   C   C
   B   B
  ACBA

The Forgotten Secret of Bibliomancy

It's common for wizards to open a magical tome at random to divine according to the first word or sentence the eye lights upon. Even the unenchanted practice this sort of bibliomancy, using whatever book they consider most sacred. But there is a subtlety that almost everyone has forgotten, and it is the one thing that ensures magical success. *The consulted book must have fallen down from a shelf on its own.* Only a book that presents itself of its own accord will be wholly reliable for consultation. Here is the procedure:

1. Once a book has fallen,
   a. pick it up respectfully
   b. dust it off gently
   c. hold it to your heart for several moments.
2. Place the book upon a table, balanced on its spine.
3. Allow the pages to fall open.
4. Close your eyes and place a finger upon the open pages.
5. Allow your finger to move across and around the pages until it seems to stop on its own.
6. Open your eyes to see what word or sentence your finger has selected.

A Riddle for
Magical Thinking

Here is an ancient riddle of wizardry. Pondering it will help to develop your magical thinking. First, we'll reveal the riddle, and then we'll offer two intriguing clues. Reflect upon this:

> The beginning of eternity,
> the end of time and space.
> The beginning of every end,
> the end of every place.
> What is it?

The riddle is usually arranged carefully, with arrows.

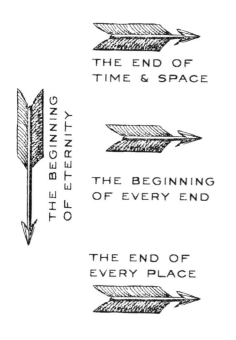

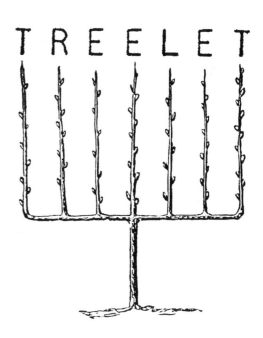

Clue number one: A treelet's twigs entwine the answer.
Clue number two: It is Merlin's only second.
Turn the page when you're ready to check your answer.

We sense that you were looking right at the answer all along. Taking the riddle one line at a time, the beginning of (the word) "eternity" is the letter E. At the end of "time" and "space" is the letter E. The beginning of every "end" and the end of every "place" is the letter E. When we rearrange the twigs of TREELET, they spell "letter E." And Merlin's only second (letter) is E.

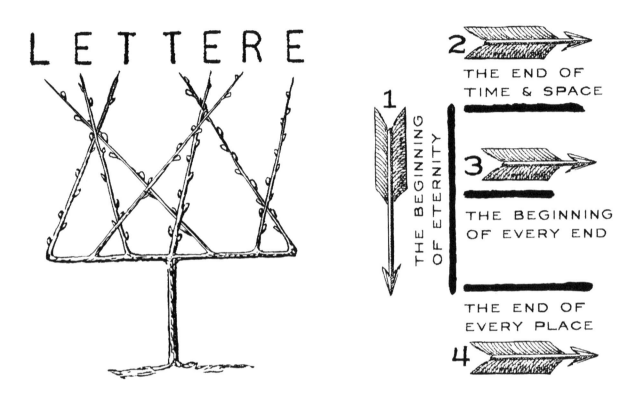

The letter E is its own wizard of words, of course, silently transforming one's cap into a cape on a chilly night, or perhaps transfiguring one's pet back into Pete (none too soon, we might add).

There's one certain way to bring the silent E to life. Offer it a breath, and it will surely breathe.

Activation
Words and Spells

Aemaet

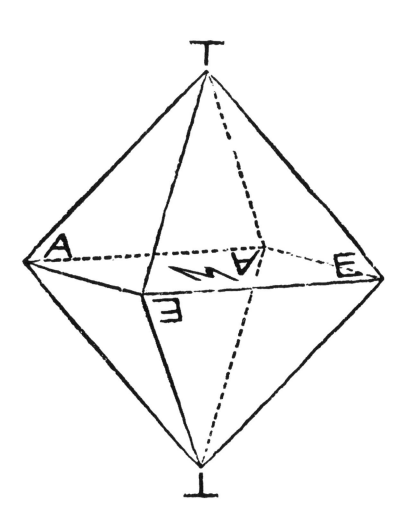

Aemaet will bring a clay figure (*golem*) to life if the word is inscribed on an amulet and then placed upon the figure. The moment the amulet is removed, the creature will become inanimate. The word, of Hebrew origin, may be translated as "truth." It is ascribed to King David and appears in the Book of Psalms.

Agimagilataragi

Of Farsi origin, *Agimagilataragi* is a general purpose magic word that will trigger any sort of occurrence the wizard wishes. It is best pronounced *Ah-gee ma-gee la-ta ra-gee*. Many wizards use this word similarly to *Ab-a-ra-ca-da-ba-ra*, when the power of an eighth syllable is required.

Animovividus Homonivalis

Animovividus Homonivalis is a Latin spell for bringing a snowman to life. This spell will gain popularity through the efforts of a wizard who will specialize in bringing an entire household to animated life, even from great distances and even without the use of a magic wand.

The word *animo* refers to the life force or vital spirit of the snowman, which is conjured to vivify with the word *vividus*. *Nivalis* means "snowy," and homo means "man." We recommend intoning this spell when snowflakes are *not* present in the air, and especially not during a blizzard, lest the snowman come to life with no sign of higher consciousness and require further magical intervention! Ambient snowflakes are to be avoided because, as hexagonal crystal prisms, they tend to refract magical glimmers and beams.

By the way, after centuries of debate, the currently favored philosophy is that magic exhibits properties of *both* glimmers and beams. Glimmers have beaming qualities, and vice versa, depending on how they're tested. (This begs a question: what is magic before it is tested?) For magic to be both a glimmer and a beam is a paradox, but accepting paradox allows us to break past the limits of what is possible and do the impossible. That's why PARADOXICAL rearranges into A RADICAL POX, because what appears to be a troublesome (poxy) conflict is in fact far-reaching and curative (radical).

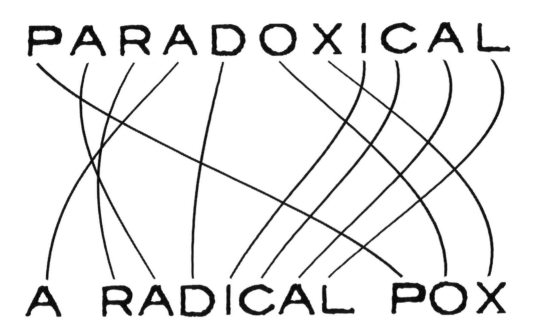

Khabs Am Pekht

This magic phrase literally means "attainment of the heavenly body." Figuratively, it is like a blessing: "May light be extended in abundance upon you." The Egyptian word *Khabs* refers to a star or lamp, while *Pekht* means to reach or attain. A simpler translation is, "Light is strength." The phrase has been traced back to the ancient Greek Hierophants of the Eleusinian Mysteries, who used it as a benediction meaning, "be vigilant; be innocent."

Khabs Am Pekht is useful for revealing a guiding star, for pulling the moon or sun out from behind a dark cloud, for bringing evidence to light, and for illuminating something previously incomprehensible. If there's one magic phrase that might help you through rough patches in your homework, *Khabs Am Pekht* is it!

This simple magic square is for filling any space with glamour and for ensuring good tidings. Note how the square cleverly fits in a bonus word. At the middle of the square, the horizontal word *Gizem* (Turkish for "mystery") transforms into *Gizam* in its vertical crossing. *Gizem Gizam* is a spell that can translate as "happily ever after." You'll find this magic square preserved in no other tome.

Make it so is a magical declaration of clear-cut intent. The phrase is equivalent to *So be it* or *So mote* (from the Middle English for *may*) *it be.* Note that the letters of *Make it so* rearrange into "I ask me to"—because the greatest magical power is not granted from without but tapped from within one's wizardly self.

O Tarot Nizael Estarnas Tantarez

O Tarot Nizael Estarnas Tantarez is a magical phrase for triggering the ability to read anyone's thoughts. Yes, as clearly as we can read yours! These words were handed down through an Egyptian book called *Treasure of the Old Man of the Pyramids*, a collection of magic talismans translated from the Language of the Magi.

Pax Sax Sarax

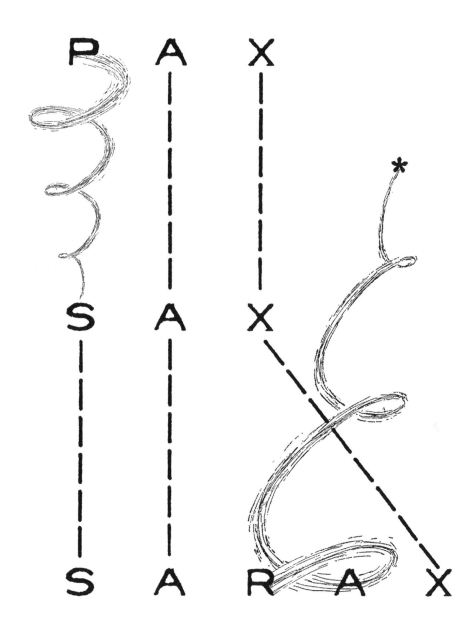

A magic spell that survives thanks to an Elizabethan manuscript, *Pax Sax Sarax* extends the duration of delightful moments. The inner workings of the spell will be obvious: *Pax* (Latin for "peace") changes to *Sax*, as the wizard alchemically transforms and takes control of the present moment; then *Sax* expands into *Sarax*, lengthening time. Note that the added syllable is *Ra*, the Egyptian sun deity, to ensure that the prolonged enjoyment is golden.

Handed down from the legends of Brittany, *Pif Paf Poof* is a spell for sending a cat away, such as when the cat is spying on behalf of a rival wizard. *Pif* and *Paf* are names of the country where cats orginated as well as the homeland of the Breton fairies.

Pon Chiki Non Non

A spell from India, *Pon Chiki Non Non* will remove whatever thing in the environment happens to be unsuitable. The spell was originally used to dematerialize a fish in mid-air, hence the expression "a fish out of water" for something out of place.

Ridas Talimol

No, *Ridas Talimol* is not an anti-headache spell. It's for commanding the elements. The words are preserved in *Treasure of the Old Man of the Pyramids* (see above). Practice using the spell to control two elements at a time. For example, control dust (earth) and air to sweep a cobblestone path, or water and air to evaporate a spill, or fire and air to warm up your study chamber.

Shazam comes with a built-in puff of smoke. Tracing its origins back to Ancient Egypt—perhaps as the name of a sorcerer—*shazam* retains the power of a lightning bolt. When spoken, this mysterious, musical word takes flight as if blown by the wind, with a hard *shhh*. Then it sizzles with the electrical *zzz*, before slamming home with the final *am*. *Shazam* promises highly dramatic magic: a flash of light, a thunderous clap, a billowing cloud, and ripples of astonishment. *Shazam!*

    The word can activate a materialization or a disappearance. It can spark a flash of insight or inspiration. It can cause an explosion or a burst of light. The word is popularly believed to be an acronym of six elder gods and heroes who bestow great powers: Solomon (wisdom), Hercules (strength), Achilles (courage), Zeus (control), Atlas (stamina) and Mercury (speed).

Tamâghis Ba'dàn Yaswàdda
Waghdàs Nawfanà Ghàdis

TAMÂGHIS

BA'DÂN

YASWÂDDA

WAGHDÂS

NAWFANÂ

GHÂDIS

Apparently of Aramaic origin, this magic spell is ascribed to the Spanish astronomer Abu al-Qasim al-Qurtubi al-Majriti. The spell, taken as a compound word, is known as "the dream word of perfect nature." It is to be said upon falling asleep, to clear the way for triggering supernatural perception and wish-fulfillment.

Note the syllables underlined: Tamàghis Ba'dàn Yaswàdda Waghdàs Nawfanà Ghàdis. Those are the inner workings of the spell. Indeed, intoning just these sounds before falling asleep will be sufficient: *Ta-ma-ba-da-ya-wa-da-wa-da-na-fa-na-ha*. Sleep tight, and magic dreams to you!

After all these *Ab-A-Ra-Ca-Da-Ba-Ra*s and *Pax Sax Saraxes*, the phrase "what if" doesn't sound much like a spell, does it? Nonetheless, the magic words "what if" are an open-sesame to a world where anything is possible. The words call upon the wizard to question the rational and expand the limits of what is possible. Like a poet who lets the imagination flow and creates miracles on paper, the wizard asks *what if* this or that could happen and then allows the magic to take effect. In our illustration, the magic words are paired with the auspicious symbol of "the mirror," one of Taoism's Eight Precious Things of good fortune.

How to Use a Talking Board to Learn New Magic Words

We predict that talking boards will one day become a parlor game for the unenchanted. The letters will be listed on the boards in alphabetical order, as everyone will have forgotten the importance of arranging the entire alphabet into a concise spell. For the time being, the talking board remains a well-kept secret of wizardry.

For the purpose of discovering new magic words, we recommend a talking board with the following spell dedicated to an amulet of Ancient Egyptian origin: "Sphinx of black quartz, judge my vow." As you will see, every letter of the alphabet appears in the spell:

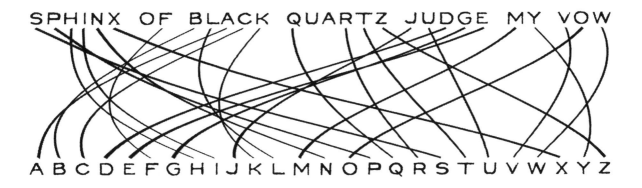

SPHINX OF BLACK QUARTZ JUDGE MY VOW

A B C D E F G H I J K L M N O P Q R S T U V W X Y Z

Spirit-writing was first recorded in China. Taoist priests used a planchette during a trance state to reveal characters written in incense ashes. Today, wizards still use the planchette, having replaced ashes with the talking board.

Rest your planchette upon the board, touch it lightly with your fingertips, and simply allow it to dance across the letters of its own accord. Note where it pauses as it spells out the magic word or spell you seek.

Here is another talking board in which every letter of the alphabet appears:

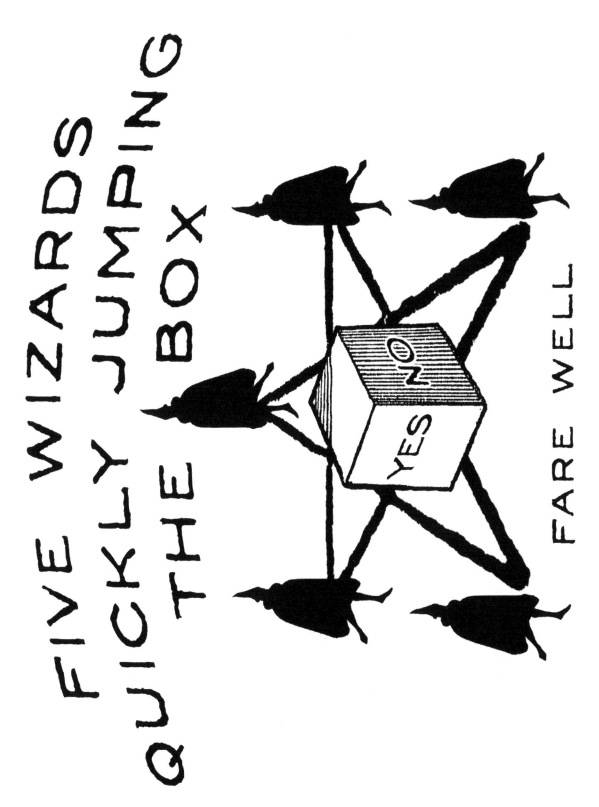

FIVE WIZARDS QUICKLY JUMPING THE BOX

FARE WELL

Protective Words and Spells

Ada Ada Io Ada Dia

Handed down from the Welsh Romany gypsies, this magic spell calls upon the forces of good fortune during challenging times. Probably of Celtic origin, the words are pronounced, *Ah-daw ah-daw eye-oh ah-daw dee-ah*. The spell was originally used for good luck in games of dice, but it will charm any circumstance.

AEEIOUO
EEIOU
EIO
IO
I

The wizards of Ancient Egypt discovered the primal power of the vowel sounds to concentrate protective supernatural forces. *Aeeiouo* is comprised of the seven sacred vowels of the Greek alphabet: Alpha, Epsilon, Eta, Iota, Omicron, Upsilon, and Omega. The spell is written in the shape of what the Egyptians considered "the self-begotten soul." (This is according to the *Nag Hammadi Library*, a collection of fifty ancient papyrus texts on the mystical meanings of the letters of the alphabet and their relation to the human spirit.) It is traditional to elongate every vowel sound as you intone this spell, as if singing. Use *Aeeiouo* to introduce and boost the power of any magic word.

Agla is an entire spell condensed into a single word, making it highly useful for talismans and seals. Of Hebrew origin, the word conjures the mysterious, unpronounceable name of the primal nature of the cosmos. The letters of *Agla* are an acronym for *Ateh Gibor Le-olam Adonai*, meaning "Yours is the power throughout endless ages, O Supreme Being."

As a word of protection, *Agla* must be spoken through the heart as well as by the tongue. The best way to accomplish this is to practice silently concentrating on your heart as you think the word *Agla* in time with your heartbeats.

All Will Be Well, and All Will Be Well, and All Manner of Things Will Be Well

This magical proclamation originated with the Medieval mystic Lady Julian of Norwich. It is an excellent spell for talismanic experimentation, as the words can be spread apart and recombined into new arrangements. The great secret of protection spells is that safekeeping and guidance can manifest in any number of ways—often in ways a wizard cannot imagine beforehand. So spreading out the words opens up more possibilities for the best outcome to work itself out. Here is an example of *All will be well, and all will be well, and all manner of things will be well* recombined and unfurled.

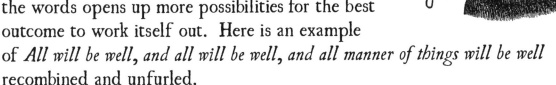

WILL   ALL   WELL

&   BE   BE   BE

ALL   THINGS   WELL

&   MANNER   ALL

WELL   THINGS

WILL   OF   WILL

Here's another example of the same spell recombined. You will recognize the shape as the "wing form."

```
W I L L
              BE
W E L L
              &     ALL
W I L L                        THINGS
              BE    ALL                      MANNER  OF
W E L L                        THINGS
              &     ALL
W I L L
              BE
W E L L
```

And here's a handy tip for wizards on the go: when space on the parchment is limited, the spell can always be condensed into sigil form.

Alu

Alu is a magic word of protection, composed of three Norse runes: *Ansuz,* *Lagus,* and *Uruz.* The rune *Ansuz* calls upon the Old Norse pantheon (including the Allfather of the gods, Odin, credited with bringing poetry and magic to humankind). The rune *Lagus* refers to water or a lake. The rune *Uruz* refers to a wild ox called an aurochs. Taken together, the runes conjure the strength and stability of an ox, the ability to flow around obstacles like water, and the guidance and support of the most high beings who safeguard humanity. *Alu* could, in fact, be translated as "holy cow."

Circulus Rotundus

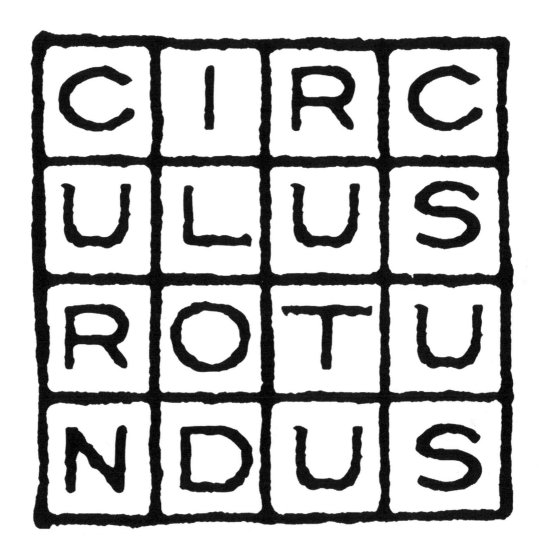

Circulus Rotundus is Latin for "round circle" and instantly creates a magic circle of protection when one cannot be traced on the ground. Note that the talismanic form of this spell is a grid of *squares*. This is a visual reference to the alchemical quest to "square the circle," a metaphor for achieving the impossible, for fusing matter and spirit.

COINCI DENTIA OPPOSI TORUM

This Latin spell reconciles any opposing forces. It was preserved by the philosopher Nicholas of Cusa. The spell solves disagreements and restores friendly relations between rivals. Its fusion of opposites recalls the Hermetic axiom, "As above, so below."

Dux Rex Lux Lex

Of Latin origin, this protective spell calls upon a luminary to guide a commandment. *Dux* refers to a leader. *Rex* means "king." *Lux* is light. And *Lex* means "law." Read as a sentence, *Dux rex lux lex* could translate as "Ruler of light, preside over the law." This is a spell to ensure fair play.

To protect private information from being revealed, the Latin spell is *Indocilis Privata Loqui*. The phrase translates as "not apt to disclose secrets." It traces back to Caesar Augustus and will become the motto of a great magic circle society.

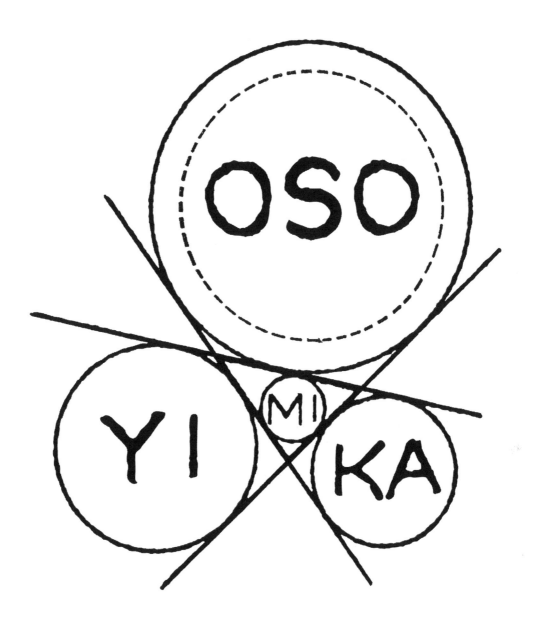

When serious reinforcements are called for, *Oso Yi Mi Ka* is an emergency magic spell from Nigeria that surrounds the wizard with circles of protective shamans. As you'd imagine, even a single circle of protective shamans is very likely to help—and it *certainly* can't hurt.

Serpens Aut Draco Qui Caudam Devoravit

Serpens aut draco qui caudam devoravit is a Latin phrase meaning a primordial serpent or dragon who swallows its own tail. (Even the greatest wizards have never learned what it does as a follow-up.) Such a creature is also known as the Ouroboros of wisdom that protects and encircles everything. It is the soul of the world and guardian of the magic formula that bestows supernatural power equal to that of the gods. Plato described this serpent as the first living thing.

The Ouroboros is a symbol of self-sufficiency, re-creating or re-inventing oneself, the eternal unity of all things, and infinity. It first emerged in Ancient Egypt, recorded in Tutankhamun's *Enigmatic Book of the Netherworld*. It later became an important symbol in alchemy, Hermeticism, and the magical talismans and emblems of Roman times. It is equivalent to Jörmungandr, the world serpent of Norse mythology which surrounds the earth and which will bring about the end of the world when it lets go of its tail.

Symplocarpus Foetidus

SYMPLOCARPUS FOETIDUS

Symplocarpus foetidus is Latin for a beautiful magical herb with a deceptively ugly name: skunk cabbage! Wizards deliberately popularized this stinky name to dissuade the unenchanted from picking and using the herb. Carrying the flower as a talisman or speaking its Latin name bestows good fortune.

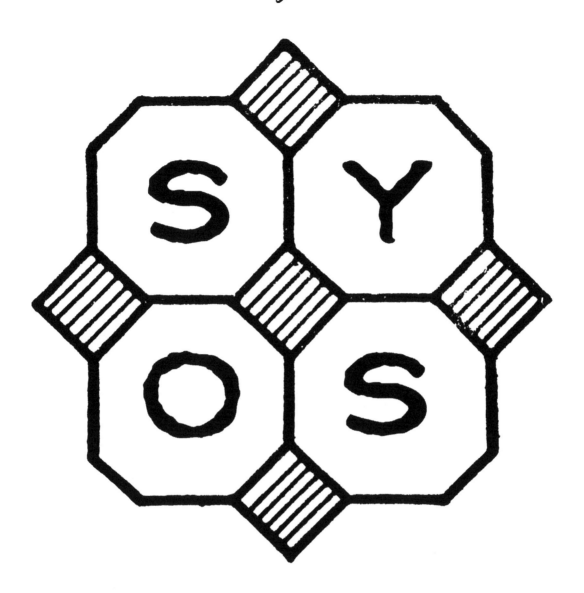

Syos is a magical invocation of the cardinal directions (North, South, East, and West). Tracing back to wizards of the High Middle Ages, the word is pronounced *sigh-ohs*. It is a concise way of establishing a space of magical protection during a time of difficulty, when it isn't convenient to invoke the angelic names of the directional guardians, *Michael*, *Gabriel*, *Raphael*, and *Uriel*.

Tien Ling Ling, Dee Ling Ling, Bien

Tien is Chinese for "celestial" or "heavenly." *Ling* is magical power. *Dee* (or *di*) refers to a mighty power, literally "Lord on High." *Bien* (or *bian*) means "expedient." Note that the magical power of *Ling* is twice doubled in this spell. The ideograms on the talisman read, from the top right down, *Tien Ling Ling Dee Ling Ling Bien.* The top center and bottom center of the talisman repeat the magic word *Ling.*

ZOLDA
OCARD
LABAL
DRACO
ADLOZ

This palindromic magic word square resolves conflicts or distresses of any sort. The words read the same left to right, bottom to top, top to bottom, and backwards. *Zolda* is from a German word meaning "peacekeeper." *Ocard* is a fairy name. *Labal*, which crosses the square vertically and horizontally, is the occult name for the revealer of all the mysteries of the Earth. *Draco* is a Latin name for a dragon. *Zolda* reversed is *Adloz*, the mirror of peace and a code word for *humility*. Taken together, the words of this spell conjure the peacekeepers of the fairy kingdom to reveal the mysterious mirror of tranquility that is guarded by a dragon.

By the way, we sense that you didn't quite catch the palindromic magic word hidden in the bottom left diagonal: *Arbra*, short for *Arbracadarbra*, a lesser-known variation of *Abracadabra*. Don't worry—you weren't *supposed* to notice it. Still, it's a good reminder to look at things obliquely.

How to Learn a New Magic Word From a Wishing Well

The unenchanted think that throwing a coin into a well is the key to having a wish granted, but we wizards know better. We know a well can do nothing with gold. Likewise, rivers give up their gold freely to those who will sift their sands. So let's be logical about this. Close your eyes and ask yourself what it is that a wishing well *wants*.

Exactly! A gift of *water* will increase the "well-being" of a wishing well. We recommend collecting water very deliberately for this purpose.

Place a copper bowl outside during a gentle rain shower. (Too stormy a shower will make for tempestuous water and will unsettle the wishing well.) Collect as much water as you can hold in your cupped hands.

Approach the wishing well in a spirit of friendliness and generosity. You come not to *take* from the well, as most do, but to *give*. Lovingly trickle your offering of water into the well, then carefully lean forward and listen for the well's voice to rise from the depths. This is the one and only way to learn new magic words from a wishing well.

Essential Single Word Spells

Anthropropolagos

Anthro comes from the Greek word for "human." *Propo* recalls the French expression *à propos*, meaning "by the way," "naturally," or "connected to what has gone before." *Lagos* is a Greek word meaning *hare*, the trickster of folklore and the reliable animal companion to magicians. *Lagos* also recalls the Greek *logos*, meaning "word." Hence, we can translate *Anthropropolagos* two ways: "I am human by way of language" and "Man and rabbit are naturally connected." A magician famous for breaking chains will spread this magic word. For the time being, it remains a wizardly secret for establishing a mental link with your hare from a distance.

Bifurcus

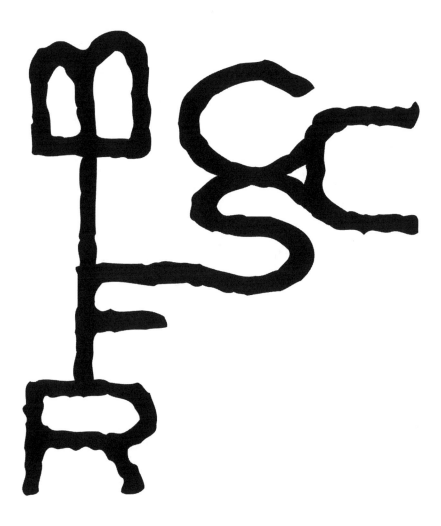

A Latin word meaning "two-forked," *bifurcus* is a spell for pinpointing the source of malicious gossip. It renders the "first tongue" of this gossip chain serpent-like (literally a forked tongue).

Excelsior

Excelsior is of Latin origin, *ex* meaning "beyond" and *celsus* meaning "lofty." Pronounced *ex-cell-see-ore*, it is a charm for gaining the upper hand when you're feeling disadvantaged, out of control, or unfairly dominated. It is a cry of ever–upward ascendancy, of supreme mastery, and of greatness. As you intone this magic word, it may help to imagine a shooting star.

    A great poet will one day exclaim that the silvery tones of *excelsior* put a soul in every bell to triumph over the powers of hell. If your intention is to inspirit a bell so as to combat a fiendish entity, be sure to allow the *el* at the center of *excelsior* to reverberate like a bell.

Gabbatha

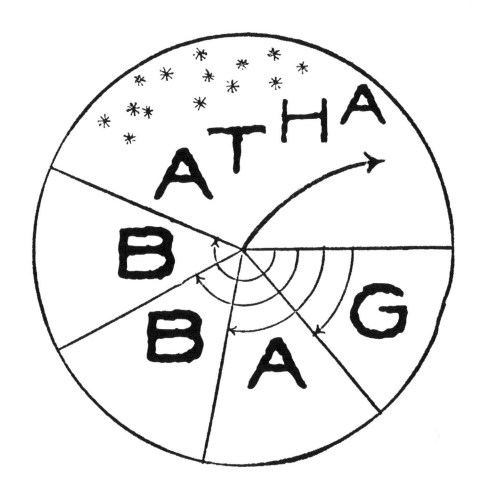

Gabbatha is a magic word for levitating heavy objects. Pronounced *gab-bath-ah*, the word is of Aramaic origin and can be translated as "elevation." (In the New Testament, *Gabbatha* appears as the name for the raised platform of Pilate's judgment seat.)

Gabbatha can also be spoken as an entreaty to raise oneself back up (similar to *Excelsior*), such as after a discouraging experience or setback. Think of it as a one-word pep talk to yourself!

Another meaning for the word is "open space," as in the wide perspective offered by a high vantage point. Therefore, *Gabbatha* is useful for gaining a sense of proportion so that you can understand the relative importance of things. It's an antidote to narrow-mindedness. It's the moment of clarity when everything "clicks," and you see that the whole is greater than the sum of its parts.

Helion

The magic word *Helion* (hee-lee-on) is derived from the Greek *helios*, referring to the Sun. *Helion* is a name for the supreme light of nature, appearing in the scrolls attributed to Moses and the mystical ciphers of Kabbalah. It is used to dispel any sort of darkness, whether of nighttime, wickedness, or an impenetrable enigma. Helion begins the magic spell *Helion Melion Tetragrammaton,* which conjures the unpronounceable celestial name at the foundation of all existence. *Tetragrammaton* is Greek for "the four letters" which constitute the most powerful magic word imaginable.

Inspiratus

The magic word *inspiratus* is Latin for the celestial "breath" that inspires creativity. Pronounced *in-spear-ah-twos*, the word is crucial during any imaginative enterprise. It is also useful when imparting an idea or illuminating a truth to someone.

A delightful fakir's incantation incorporates the word as it celebrates a paradox: "Hocus, pocus, inspiratus, there is a cat in the hat; hocus, pocus, inspiratus, there is no cat in the hat." An Austrian theorist will make a name for himself with this feline paradox about a cat which both is and isn't alive in a box. The reason the cat pops in and out of existence is related to how inspiration tends to come in flashes and how the chime of a clock can disintegrate a dream.

Ishkabibble

A fake Yiddish magic word, *Ishkabibble* sweeps away worries as efficiently as a broom sweeps away an abandoned cobweb. The spell works especially well in conjunction with a talisman of pressed flowers. (Feel free to press flowers within our pages anytime. Contrary to popular belief, the thought of pressing flowers doesn't give a book butterflies in the stomach.)

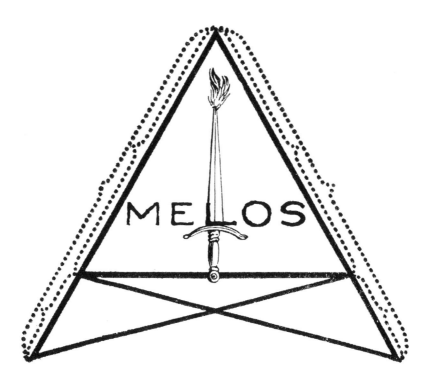

Aristotle used the word *melos* to identify the spellbinding power of incantations. Pronounced *may-lows*, the word is a charm whose rhythms have the power to compel an involuntary physical response. Therefore, it is useful in situations of standstill or stalemate, when further action or progress seems impossible. *Melos* gets things moving, against inertia.

The Ancient Greek word *Melos* literally means "music." As a magic word, the name Melos appears in the amulet parchments of Abyssinian Christianity and other Ethiopian magic texts. It refers to "the fearful sword of fire" that descends from "the gate of light."

But as with much that's magical, there is more than meets the eye here! You see, there is a secret, coded history of the word *Melos*. The Semitic magician King Solomon, who figured highly in Ethiopian mythology, is said to have considered *Melos* to be a magic

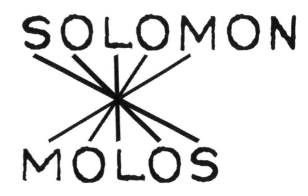

word. Note that *Melos* is a form of the name Solomon. Solomon spelled backwards is *Nomolos*, which shortens to *Molos*, and a slight vowel adjustment forms *Melos*. *Melos* is a coded reference to King Solomon in the Abyssinian liturgical texts. The word conjures his incisive wisdom—his fiery, rapier wit. And so *Melos* is helpful to get not only things but *ideas* moving.

By the way, secret coding is not the only reason for spelling words backwards. There's something much deeper at play. Wizards reverse letters so as to create the word's image in an immaterial magic mirror. A looking glass is a window into a strange, extra-dimensional world.

And so we have revealed a priceless secret: to reflect upon the profound, otherworldly significance of a word, it's best to ponder an actual *reflection* of that word. The mystical practice of reversing letters and syllables is age-old. From *Tien*, the Chinese word for heaven and fate, the Egyptians reversed the sounds into *Neith[a]*, a heavenly goddess of war; the Greeks wrote that name backwards to form *Athene*, also a goddess of war.

To give another example, the Bengali god of love is *Dipuc*, which is reversed in Latin as *Cupid*, the Roman god of love.

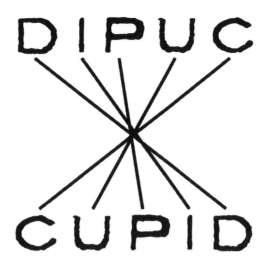

Similarly, the Coptic word *Chlom* means *crown*. The sounds of *Chlom* reverse into the Hebrew *Moloch*, meaning a king who wears a crown.

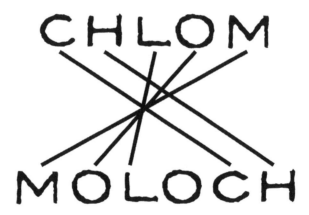

To give just one more example, the Persians called Venus *Mitra*, which the Scythians reversed into *Artim*, hence the Greek goddess *Artemis*.

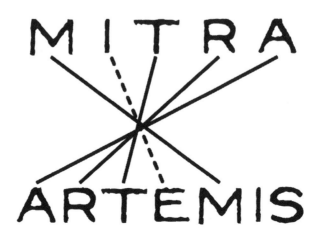

Mijoter

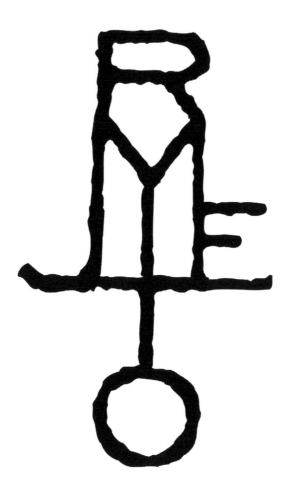

Of French origin, this magic word calls forth a subtle action about as delicate as a tiny bubble rising up and breaking on the still surface of a newly stoked cauldron. Pronounced *me-zhuh-tay*, the word's literal meaning is "to simmer." Use it when a situation calls for a persnickety approach. You're correct in thinking that the spell might not sound like much, but keep in mind that dramatic gestures aren't always appropriate or even useful. For example, both a tiny flame and a raging fireball will light a candle, but the fireball will melt the candle at once. A wizard can manipulate a great many circumstances with the tiniest shift. *Mijoter* is as effective as it is energy-efficient.

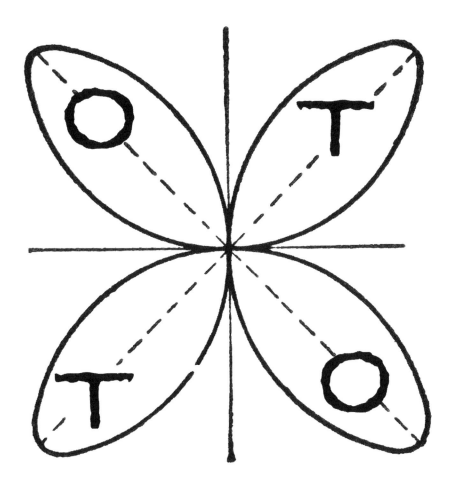

This ancient German magic word conjures prosperity. Its literal meaning is "wealth, riches." Pronounce it *ah-tow*, extending each syllable for as long as your lungs will allow. It is proper to use this word in conjunction with the essence of rose petals; that fragrant oil is also known as *otto*, and the rose is an alchemical symbol of transmutation (as in lead to gold). The reason for such symbolism is self evident when you hold a rose to your nose—as you inhale the rose's transcendent fragrance, you feel your consciousness melt into wholeness. You feel your microcosm expand into the macrocosm. As a Sufi alchemist once wrote, mystery glows in the rose bed and the secret is hidden within the petals. Indeed, the Latin phrase *sub rosa* refers to a secret and translates as "under the rose." The phrase traces back to a rose suspended from the ceiling of a council chamber, pledging all in attendance to remain quiet about the proceedings.

Qmfbtf

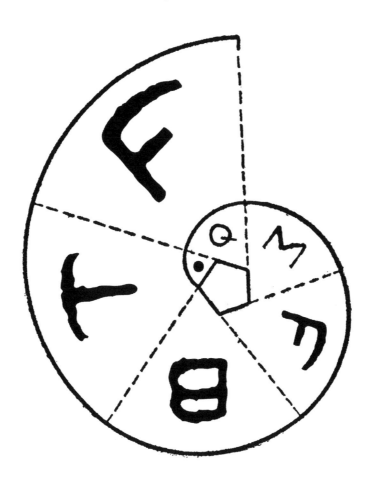

Inaudibly mumbled and whispered over the centuries, many magic words inevitably become corrupted and lose their original meanings. Yet that doesn't necessarily mean that they lose their power. Gregorian chants still have a hypnotizing effect, even after their language has fallen out of use. A mystery offers its own special kind of potency, and magic words have come to be considered effective to the degree that they are strange and incomprehensible.

Qmfbtf, like the similarly incomprehensible *Hfuhruhurr*, is a testament to the potency of mumbled syllables that carry a powerful mystery. Both words have belatedly been proven to have a calming effect on dragons. Though *Qmfbtf* may look like a mumble, it must be pronounced carefully. *Qm* sounds like "come." *Fb* is pronounced "fab." And *tf* sounds like "tough." However, for purposes of dragon taming, the word is best used in talismanic form. From a distance.

Shibumi

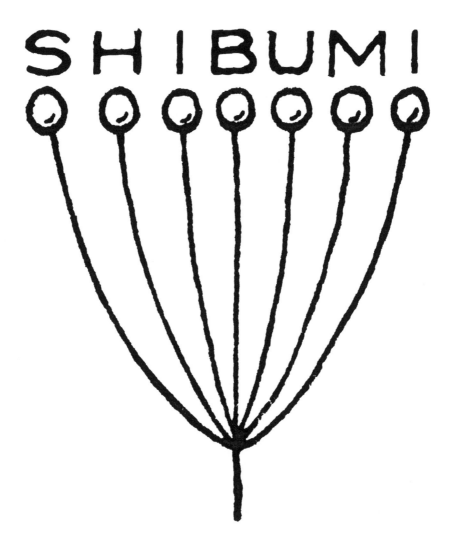

Shibumi is a Japanese word for conjuring a magical mist that effortlessly and gracefully manifests a wizard's intention. In the absence of a specific intention, *Shibumi* will grant the serenity of inner peace—which is not too shabby, in our opinion. The word is pronounced *she-boo-me.*

A Mirror of Magic Words for Restoring a Forgotten Memory

In the life of every wizard there has been at least one event which was impressive and important at the time but now is forgotten completely. It may have been something unpleasant or humorous, sacred or sad, a childhood prank, or a kind deed. Or it may have been a quotation from a beloved magical tome or from an old family saying, from an animal familiar, or from some unusal enchanter. Or it may have been any one of many other events in the life of a wizard.

We sense one such occurrence in your own life, but it is not our place to reveal it. Yet if you wish, we shall provide you with a way to bring that forgotten day to the forefront of your memory. However, we must ask you to be honest with yourself and to accept and acknowledge this most unusual phenomenon.

Our experiment is far from new and traces back to Ireland during the rule of High King Conn of the Hundred Battles, whose son Connla fell in love with a fairy and sailed to the Otherworld in a crystal boat.

It is said that the greatest wish of the fairy queen Titania is that the past shall not be forgotten. With the assistance of a magic mirror made of words, a lost memory of the past will come back, never again to be forgotten.

We will reproduce the magic mirror of words below. When you are ready, begin by making your presence known to Queen Titania by reciting the following:

Oh, Titania, our Fairy Queen
And Grace of the court of ancient dreams,
To this humble wizard before thee here
Bring back the thoughts of yesteryear.

Having recited these words, gaze into the magic mirror of words for a moment. Then close your eyes while the Queen brings back a memory of the past, never to be forgotten.

After your memory is restored, it is traditional to speak words of thanks:

Oh, Fairy Queen,
May my heart be full of cheer
And my memory of the past, and thee,
Remain forever and a year.

A smithy will one day popularize this memory restoration technique, using an enchanted goblet in place of a magic mirror.

LET
THESE
WORDS
BE
A
REMINDER

Rhyming Spells

The Great Secret of Rhyming Spells

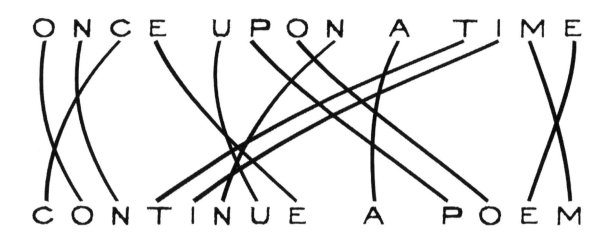

ONCE UPON A TIME

CONTINUE A POEM

There is nothing babyish about childhood rhymes and counting songs, and the reason is a great secret. These rhymes are surviving fragments of the incantations of sorcerers from ancient times. The oral tradition has preserved them even as old parchments have crumbled into dust. Unenchanted folk laugh at these rhymes, but in their mindless singsonging they transmit the code from generation to  generation. Thus great secrets remain hidden and yet protected by unknowing guardians, waiting to be recognized by those with insight. As the German magician and alchemist Heinrich Cornelius Agrippa will note, while the unbelieving and unworthy remain ignorant of their own ignorance, no secrets are concealed from the wise.

While any nursery rhyme may be used to bewitch or otherwise gain control over someone, several rhymes possess especially potent magic for specific purposes. We'll share our favorites below.

Ade milo sti milia,
Ke heretam ti griya;
Posa hronia the na ziso?
Ena, thio, tria, tesera.

This Greek rhyme is a spell for determining how many years you shall live. It conjures the crone witch guardian of the apple tree (the same hag immortalized in the fairy tale of Snow White). The rhyme can be translated: "Go apple to the apple tree, and my compliments to the old woman; how many years shall I live? One, two three, four." However, we cannot recommend using this spell. As a sparrow will one day pronounce on a strange tide in the Caribbean, it is best not to know which moment may be your last; keep every morsel of your entire being alive to the infinite mystery of it all.

ANIMA

ASA NISI MASA

This Italian spell has been preserved in the children's language game known as "la lingua serpentina" (serpentine language). The root of the spell is *Anima*, which means "soul" or "spirit" in Italian. Within that word are inserted the syllables "sa" and "si" to create a magical chant. The spell is a bridge between the present and the past. Whoever intones the words will travel back in time to rediscover a lost source of inspiration. *Asa Nisi Masa* is best pronounced *ah-saw knee-see ma-saw*.

Here is how the word *magic* can be transformed through "la lingua serpentina":

MAGIC

MASA GISI CASA

Masa Gisi Casa is best pronounced *ma-saw gee-see caw-saw*. Intoning it will instantly enchant any situation.

To give just one more example, the word *wizard* can be transformed thusly:

WIZARD

WISA ZASI RASA DASI

Wiza Zasi Rasa Dasi is best pronounced *wee-saw zaw-see raw-saw daw-see*. Intoning it will call upon the assistance of the nearest mage.

Diggi daggi, Schurry murry
Horum harum, Lirum larum
Raudi maudi, Giri gari
Posito
Besti basti, Saron froh
Fatto matto, Quid pro quo

A child prodigy will work this musical incantation into an operatic
aria. Though the exact meaning of these words is lost, the spell's power
actually lies in its enigma. The spell is a confession, of sorts: it admits
its own ignorance of the deepest secrets. The sounds are evocative, the
rhythm is precise, but the words are not literal. And so the spell has been
transformed into a poem, and poetry is magic because it stands outside of
time, breaks the rules, changes consciousness, and captures the immaterial
and makes it visible.

Eenie, meenie, tip de-dee,
Ola, dola, Dominee;
Ochre, poker, dominoca,
Hy, pon, tuss

What vestige of a magic spell can you detect in this apparent gibberish chanted by children? You're right! "Ochre, poker, dominoca" is an echo of the Latin spell "Hocus, pocus, dominocus." The *Dominee* of the second line is another form of the Latin *dominus*, meaning "Master" or "Lord." The opening words, *Eenie, meenie* (followed by *minie moe* in other popular counting rhymes) put the matter in question into the hands of fate. Those words are prehistoric, likely dating to the construction of Stonehenge. Suffice it to say that this children's verse is merely *disguised* as nonsense.

Gorgora, Behera
Chikitoun, Chakatoun
Fuera!

This is a Basque rhyme for banishing any unwanted thing. It begins with an echo of the axiom of Hermes, "As above, so below," and it ends with a casting "Out!"

Ha Ya Ba Ra La

Originating in India, *Ha Ya Ba Ra La* is unlike Abracadabra in an important way. Abracadabra is structured according to the alphabet: A-B-ra-C-a-D-abra. But *Ha Ya Ba Ra La* is disordered. It's the magic spell for mixing things up into a more interesting configuration, for breaking with tradition, and for stimulating creativity.

Hinx, spinx, the devil winks;
The fat begins to fry

Where does the magic lie in this nursery verse of yesteryear? In another version, the first line is, "Hinx, minx, the old witch winks." The tripled *X* sound of *hinx, spinx, winx* is the source of the enchantment. The rhythm is also crucial to the charm's power—note how there are six syllables in the first line, and *five* of them are stressed. It's a sign of carefully crafted language when nearly every beat counts. And where there's craft, there's purpose.

We see even more purpose by the mention of a devil or a witch— they symbolize clever, self-willed people. In the second line, the winking magically causes an instant transformation; the frying fat has a figurative meaning that things are becoming more intense, exciting, and inflamed. So this rhyme is a spell for heating things up, whether literally or figuratively. It's a good spell during cauldron stirring and garden-variety alchemy.

Ibrekh loole
Keche kule,
Ya doonda,
Ya shoonda,
Taghta kure bashenda

This children's verse from Armenia is a spell for finding out *who* is guilty of something. It can also be used to uncover a hidden object. Pronounce the *I*'s as *ee* in green, and pronounce the *A*'s as *ah*.

One-ery, two-ery, ziccary zeven
Hollow-bone, crack-a-bone, ten or eleven
Spin, spon, it must be done
Twiddledum, twaddledum, twenty-one

This rhyme, which hails from England, attracts luck when you're required to perform a task you feel uncertain about. (Gym class? Yes, it certainly *could* come in handy there.) The focus on the number twenty-one in the last line is a tripling of lucky seven. The cracking bones in the third line refers to the ossifrage, the Old World bone-crushing bird of prey.

Rata
Pata
Scata
Fata

Of Caribbean origin, with traces of Spanish and West African languages, *Rata-pata-scata-fata* is a spell for speeding time and chiming the hour. The rat of *Rata* is a close cousin of the rat in the nursery rhyme, "Hickory dickory dock, the rat ran up the clock." Incidentally, the words *hickory dickory* derive from the Romany gypsy spell *ekkeri akairi*.

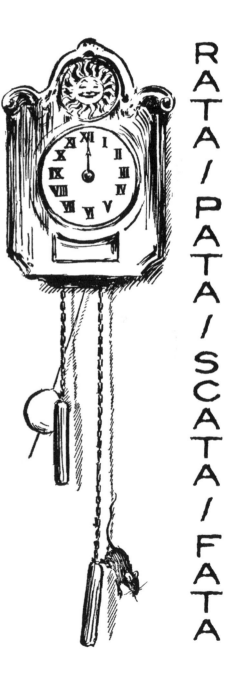

RATA / PATA / SCATA / FATA

Distilling Traditional Rhymes

You'll discover so much when you study traditional verses. One surprising insight is that a nursery rhyme can be *alchemically distilled*, its key word containing every main point. In the following example, about a protective amulet, we see that the ordered parts of a horseshoe nail serve as an outline to the story.

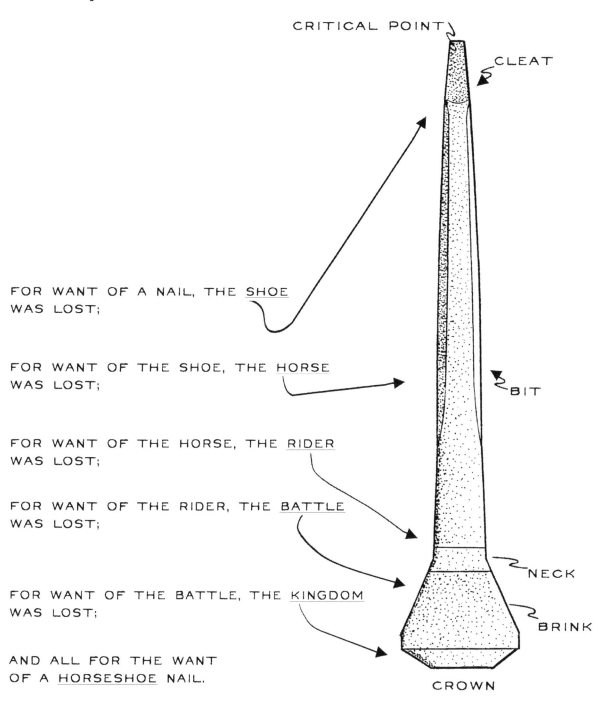

CRITICAL POINT

CLEAT

FOR WANT OF A NAIL, THE <u>SHOE</u> WAS LOST;

FOR WANT OF THE SHOE, THE <u>HORSE</u> WAS LOST;

BIT

FOR WANT OF THE HORSE, THE <u>RIDER</u> WAS LOST;

FOR WANT OF THE RIDER, THE <u>BATTLE</u> WAS LOST;

NECK

FOR WANT OF THE BATTLE, THE <u>KINGDOM</u> WAS LOST;

BRINK

AND ALL FOR THE WANT OF A <u>HORSESHOE</u> NAIL.

CROWN

By the way, traditional verses, fairy tales, myths, and legends immortalize a great many wizards whose hijinks were truly unforgettable. Though too many such stories paint our brethren in an unflattering light, we know that events are never black and white but rather silvery gray. Some notable wizards and their tales include:

* Atlantes, a powerful sorcerer who built an enchanted castle filled with illusions, in the Old French *Chanson de Geste* (song of heroic deeds).

* Farmer Weathersky (also known as Farmer Weatherbeard), a shape-shifting wizard in the Norwegian tale *Bonde Værskjegg*.

* Fioravante, who transformed himself into a man with hair and teeth of gold, in the Italian tale *Cannetella*.

* Fitcher, a wizard who possessed a special egg which was surely the transformative "philosopher's stone" of alchemy, in the German tale *Fitcher's Bird*.

* Gwydion ("Born of Trees"), a shape-shifting hero in the Fourth Branch of the Welsh tales of the *Mabinogi*.

* Jannes and Jambres, a pair of wizards who contested with Moses in the Hebrew Book of Exodus and who, in tales of the Kabbalah, used powerful talismans to journey all the way to the fifth heaven to face the archangel Metatron.

* Koschei, a wizard who flies on a whirlwind in the Russian tale *Maria Morevna and Koschei the Wizard*.

* Maestro Lattantio, a tailor who mastered wizardry in the Italian tale *Maestro Lattantio and His Apprentice Dionigi*.

* Merlin (also known as Myrddin Wyllt), the prophetic bard, court advisor, and shape-shifter in the Arthurian legends of Britain.

* Prospero, the Duke of Milan who learns sorcery from books and controls elemental creatures, in the British tale *The Tempest*.

* The Telkhines, four magician metalworkers with the power to control the weather, in the ancient Greek myths.

* Väinämöinen, a wise, magical-voiced elder in the Finnish *Kalevala*.

How to Pinpoint the Magic Word in a Stag's Antlers

Most wizards know that a stag's antlers align with a particular constellation in the night sky. It's lesser-known that the name of the brightest star of that constellation is the magic word for commanding the stag to do your bidding.

In our example, the stag's antlers point to the constellation of the Hunter and the Hounds, whose brightest star (at the Hunter's knee) is *Arcturus*. That star name, best pronounced *ark-tour-us*, is of ancient Greek origin and means "Guardian of the Bear." However, you may prefer the Inuit name of the same star, *Uttuqalualuk* (best pronounced *ooh-too-cal-ooh-all-ook*) meaning "the Old Man." Or you may prefer the Sanskrit name, *Svati* (best pronounced *sv-ah-tee*) meaning "very beneficient." These are all age-old names and will all enchant a stag with that precise configuration of branched horns.

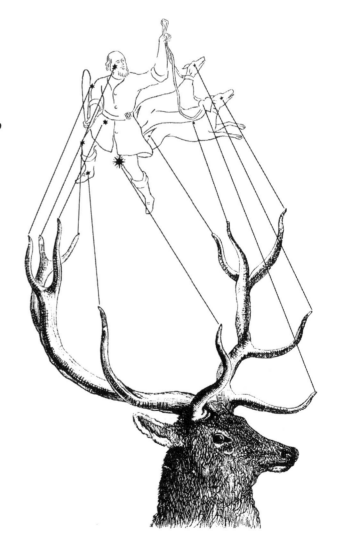

If you forget the name of particular star, simply consult a tome such as Azophi's *Book of Fixed Stars*, Ptolemy's *Almagest*, or Zhang Heng's *Spiritual Constitution of the Universe*.

Using Magic Words to Attract a Familiar

To attract a beastly familiar to do your bidding, carry on your person a talisman with a sigil of the species you feel most drawn toward. Use one of the following dog-eared but faithful sigils—or design your own!

Cat – Felinus

Crow – Corvus

Wolf – Lupus

Owl – Noctua

Toad – Bufo

Snake – Serpens

Dog – Canis

Dove – Columba

Rabbit – Lepus

Abraxas

Wyvern

Sphinx

Cocatrice

Manticore

Basilisk

Draco

Unicornis

Chimera

Amphisbaena

Griffin

How to Learn a New Magic Word from a Tree

Listening to the communication of trees is ultimately no different than listening to your animal familiar. Here are nine tips to facilitate the process:

1. If possible, return to the tree which provided the branch from which you fashioned your magic wand or staff. If you don't know or cannot access that particular tree, seek out a circle of hardwood trees in a forest and sit at the center of them.

2. Listening for magic words from trees is neither a relaxation nor a meditation exercise. It is an active *attuning* of your hearing.

3. Being respectful of arboreal nobility will enhance your ability to hear magic words.

4. Notice the rustling of leaves in the breeze and the creaking of branches. These are tree sounds but not magic words. Listen carefully *beyond* those rustlings and creakings.

5. Be patient, as both time and perseverance are typically required to hear a tree's whispered words.

6. If, after several sittings, you still aren't attuned to hearing magic words, place your ear against a tree trunk. Allow the tree's magic words to envelop you.

7. Note that your other senses may detect a tree's magic words before your ears do.

8. Though trees communicate magic words all the year through, early spring tends to be an especially talkative season.

9. Keep your ears open for unicorn sounds, too. You never know!

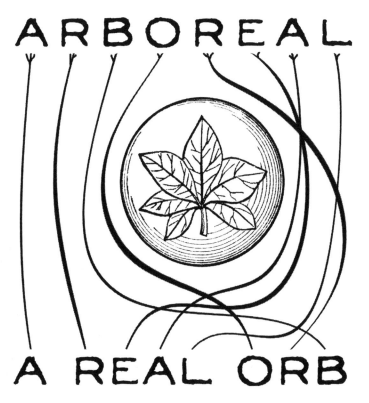

ARBOREAL

A REAL ORB

Another way to learn a new magic word from a tree is to study its fallen leaves. A great author will one day proclaim that "in every leaf a magic word is sealed." Note the runic mysteries hidden in our example below. Now you know the origin of the phrase "leafing through" the pages of a book!

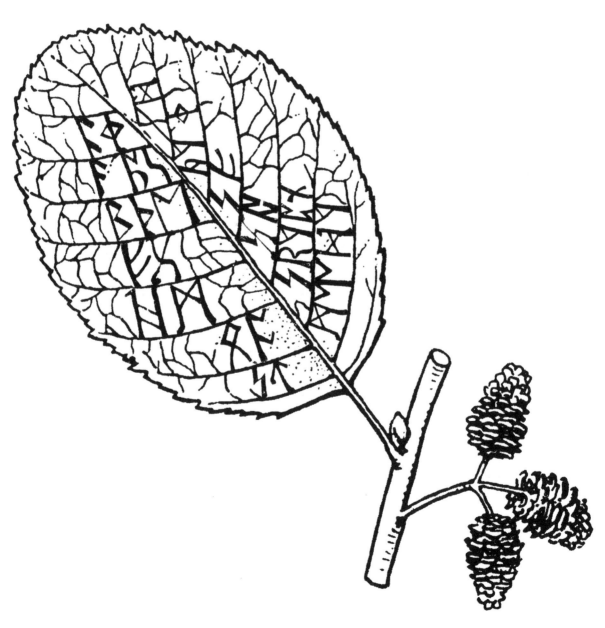

Dangerous Words and Spells

*Abacabadabacabaeabacabadabacabafabacabad-abacabae
abacabadabacabagabacabadabacabaeaba-cabadabacabaf
abacabadabacabaeabacabadabacaba*

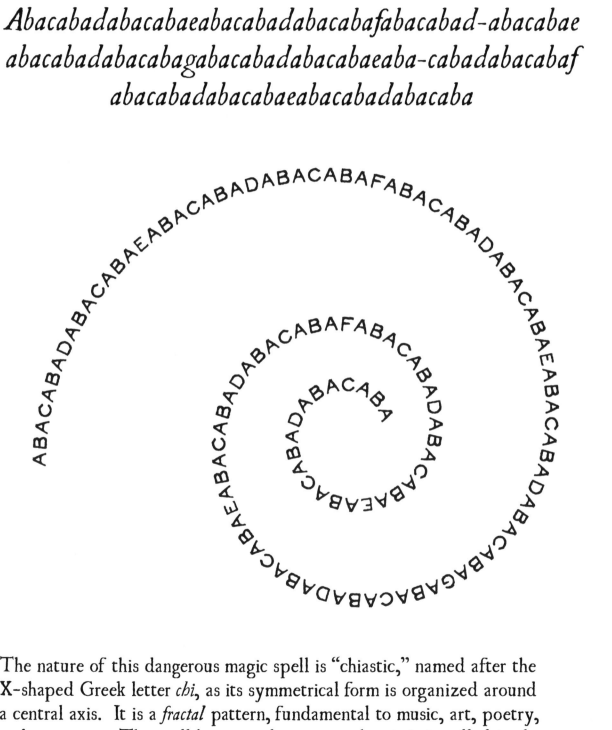

The nature of this dangerous magic spell is "chiastic," named after the
X-shaped Greek letter *chi*, as its symmetrical form is organized around
a central axis. It is a *fractal* pattern, fundamental to music, art, poetry,
and geometry. The spell becomes dangerous when it is installed in the

corners of your room, as it will trap imps. They can read in one direction only, and so they find themselves caught in the center of the spiral. As a wordsmith will exclaim, visual poetry is for catching the dark things that dwell in the back of your head and fixing them for all to see. If you don't want the world to know what mischief lies in the secret corners of your mind, never risk using this spell.

If you find that you *must* construct this spell, begin with a letter. Add the next letter of the alphabet. Then repeat everything that came before the new letter. So if you begin with A, adding the next letter, B, forms AB, then repeating what came before the new letter creates ABA. Continue by adding the next letter, C, and repeating that which came before, namely ABA. That makes ABA-C-ABA. Then add the letter D and repeat the pattern to form ABACABA-D-ABACABA. Adding E to the chain creates ABACABADABACABA-E-ABACABADABACABA. Adding F creates ABACABADABACABAEABACABADABACABA-F-AB ACABADABACABAEABACABADABACABA. And so on.

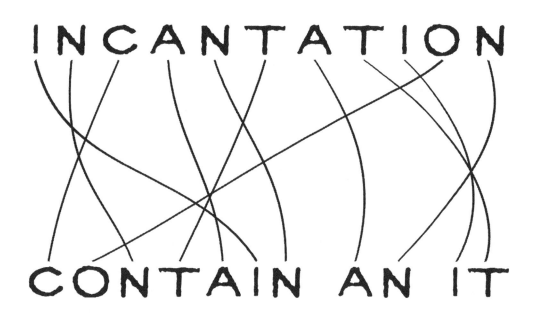

Kedavra

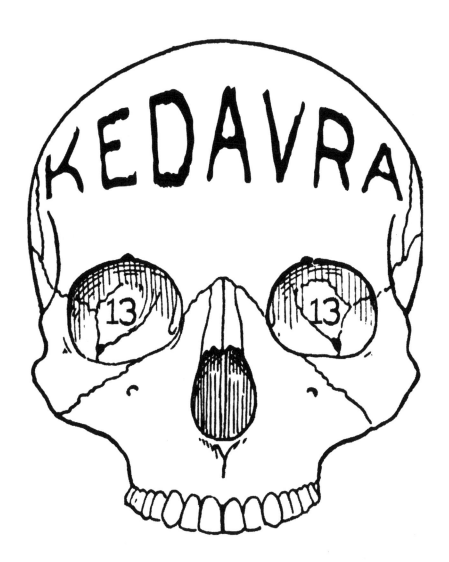

Even more than its cousin *cadabra*, the magic word *kedavra* is shrouded by an ominous, dark aura of necromancy. Even simply thinking the word conjures a cadaver in your subconscious! The Latin root of the word means "to fall."

Kedavra is dangerous, but not for the reason you are thinking. Recall the old proverb, "To kill another is to dig your own grave." There is truth in that. To kill another is to slay a part of yourself. There are many things more powerful than killing. Ponder, if you will: it is more powerful to disrupt than to kill. It is more powerful to influence than to kill. It is more powerful to understand than to kill. It is more powerful to forgive than to kill. It is more powerful to love than to kill.

Perciphedron

Perciphedron is a magic word written in white letters on the belly of a magical fish named "Kron-zhig," who lies on the bottom of the ocean and emerges from the deep every century to shriek her own name. (Some creatures will do *anything* for publicity.) *Perciphedron* conjures a comet tail, which is extraordinarily dangerous. Think about it: a comet combines the elements of ice and fire. Even if you are talented at controlling the elements, ice-fire separates the masters from the novices. The last wizard who conjured with *Perciphedron* was hit in the solar plexus by the comet and turned to bronze. Uncannily, his tongue clapped against his palate like a bell and sent deafening ringing echoes. A Bulgarian poet will immortalize the magical fish Kron-zhig and the dangerous magic word *Perciphedron*.

Satom Agemo Tenet Omega Motas

SATOM
AGEMO
TENET
OMEGA
MOTAS

Satom is a Mundari word meaning "after two years." (Reciting it can help a wizard obtain an associate's degree.) *Agemo* is the shape-shifting chameleon of Yoruba lore. *Tenet* is a Latin word meaning *holds, keeps, comprehends, possesses, masters, preserves.* *Omega* is the final letter of the Greek alphabet, symbolizing finality and endings. *Motas* is a magic word preserved by the Roman statesman Marcus Porcius Cato.

The reason this palindromic magic word square is dangerous will be quite obvious even to a complete novice. To place irreversible endings into the hands of a shape-shifting chameleon is a recipe for torment. The fact that this spell has a time-delay of two years makes it seem less dangerous. But recall the adage, "Bewitch beforehand, regret afterward."

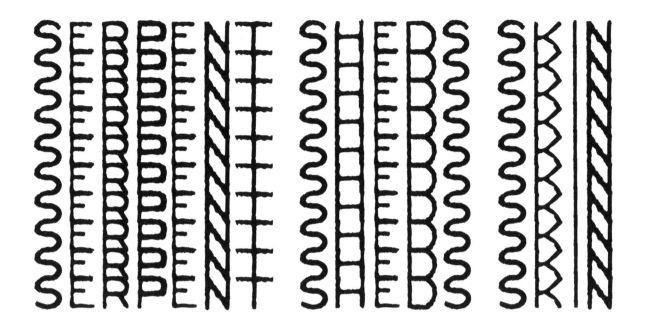

This tongue-twister of a spell, to be spoken quickly ten times in a row, poses a temporary danger but is otherwise very positive. The spell effectively triggers growth and new beginnings. The danger lies in the fact that when a serpent sheds its skin, it is temporarily rendered blind. Thus a wizard who intones this spell will, for a short time, become visually impaired or otherwise unmindful. The wizard will experience being easily overwhelmed and careless. This is not a spell to use while gazing into the future, while standing on a precipice, or while controlling heavy objects.

Siweklach

Preserved in the fairy tales of Austria, this ancient magic word calls upon the assistance of the phoenix. The word is pronounced *sigh-weck-lock*. As a conjured phoenix will rise from flames, be very careful not to speak *Siweklach* in the presence of anything flammable! The last time a wizard pronounced the word was during a time of drought, when the underbrush and grass were dry as tinder. The flames lept from tree to tree until they lit up the whole horizon, all the way to Gray Face Mountain. The sky was so full of smoke that the unenchanted could stare at the sun without blinking. It took a century for the forest to renew itself, though the rattlenakes never did return.

Talitha, Kum

Talitha, kum is an Aramaic phrase used in incantations to raise the dead. Necromancy of this sort is strongly discouraged. The difficulty is not in reinvigorating the dead but rather in maintaining command once they arise.

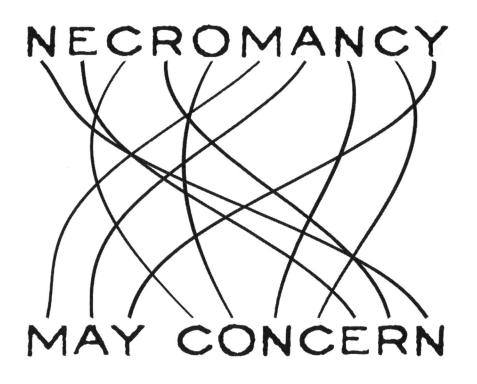

The Nine Aspects of a Magic Word

The ancient Egyptians saw the human body and soul as containing nine parts. The same is true of each and every magic word. This understanding of the nine aspects of magic words, known through the science of *taxonomy*, is available to highly advanced wizards. Yet we sense that you are ready for an introduction to the deepest dimensions of magical language. Exactly where this knowledge will take you, only time will tell.

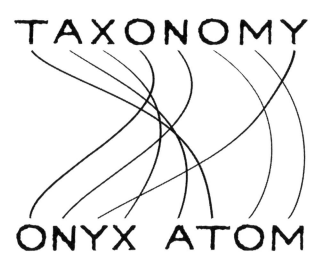

1. Kha (sometimes spelled Khat): This is the physical form of the magic word—the ink on parchment—that can decay over time unless entombed in amber.

2. Sahu: This is the immaterial aspect of the magic word that can never decay. When we trace magic words in the air, it is the Sahu that is activated.

3. Ka: This is the magic word's "double" that lingers on in a talisman after the spell is completed.

4. Ba: This is the winged "spirit" of the magic word that travels when a spell must cover a great distance.

5. Khu (sometimes spelled Akhu, Akh, Ikhu): This is the radiant, eternal aspect of the magic word. It carries the will and intentions of the spell in a point of light.

6. Khaibit: This is the "shadow" of the magic word. All luminosity creates a shadow, and the brighter the magic, the deeper the shadow.

7. Sekhem: This is the force or power that energizes the magic word.

8. Ab (sometimes spelled Ib): This is the "heart" of the magic word, concerned with higher principles of right and wrong.

9. Ren: This is the true, secret name of the magic word. Without a secret name, a magic word is merely make-believe.

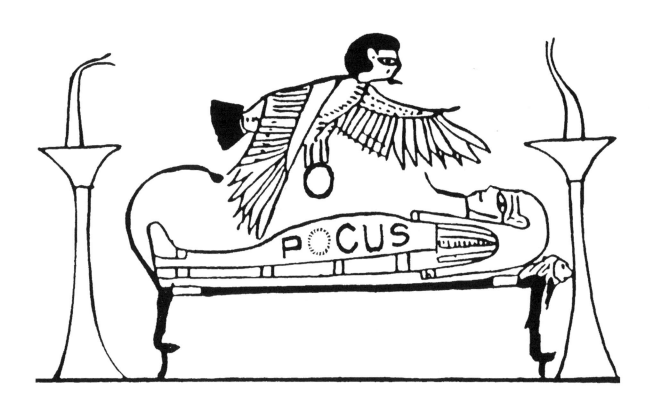

How to Build a Memory Palace for Magic Words

Because so many magic words and spells feature intricate lettering and phrasing, a wizard benefits from memory tricks. We know you sometimes have trouble remembering things—people's names, where you put your toadstone, what time the moon rises—but that's okay. This will help. The Memory Palace is a *mnemonic device* preserved in the

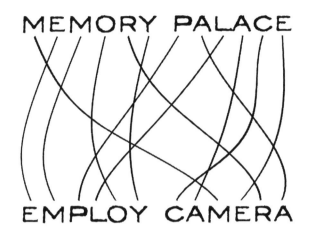

oldest surviving Latin book on rhetoric, *Rhetorica ad Herennium*. Here are nine steps for building your own memory palace so that you can have a limitless storehouse of magic words at the tip of your tongue:

1. The wizard visualizes a favorite palace or imagined locale. The larger and more detailed the space, the more magic words you can store in your memory.

2. Be sure that each room or area within the palace is distinct. That way one location can't be mistaken for another.

3. As the words of magic spells are remembered in a certain order, plot a route for mentally traveling through your memory palace.

4. Place images of letters, syllables, words, or sigils in specific rooms within your memory palace. When you mentally walk through the palace, you will observe what has been placed where.

5. Don't put too much in any one room. A single letter, syllable, or symbol is sufficient. And, by all means, mind your feng shui!

6. Give defining characteristics to each letter or symbol you place, such as a color, a size, and even a scent. The more detail you provide, the more memorable each element will be.

7. In cases of exceptionally long magic words or spells, fit more information within a room by visualizing smaller locations such as pieces of furniture and paintings on the walls. Use as many of these as you need to store your images.

8. To help further establish your memory palace in your mind, draw a blueprint which shows the locations of the magical elements.

9. The more you mentally explore your palace, the more easily you will recall its magic spells on demand.

Here's an example of a memory palace floor plan which stores the lettering of two magic words: the protection spell *Zephaniah* and the tongue-twisting command of attraction, *Tirratarratorratarratirratarratum*.

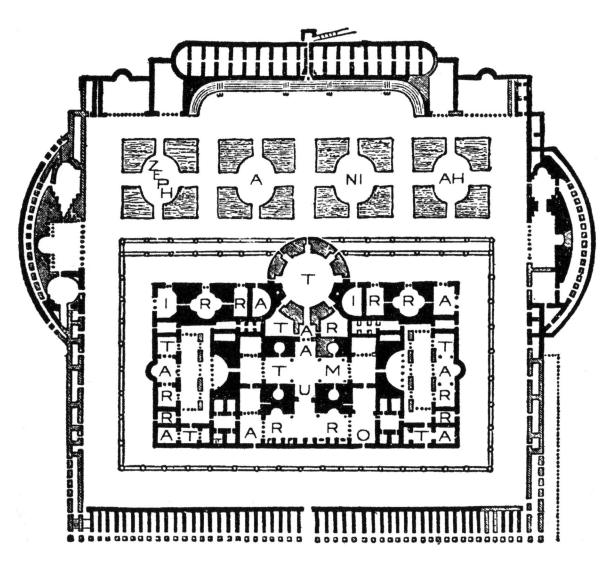

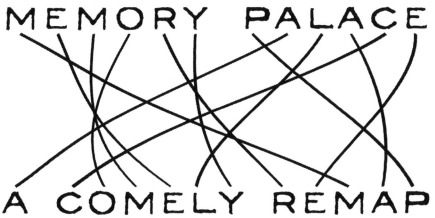

Here's a memory palace floor plan for remembering the lettering of *Tetragrammaton*, the most powerful magic word imaginable. (You wouldn't want to forget *that* one!)

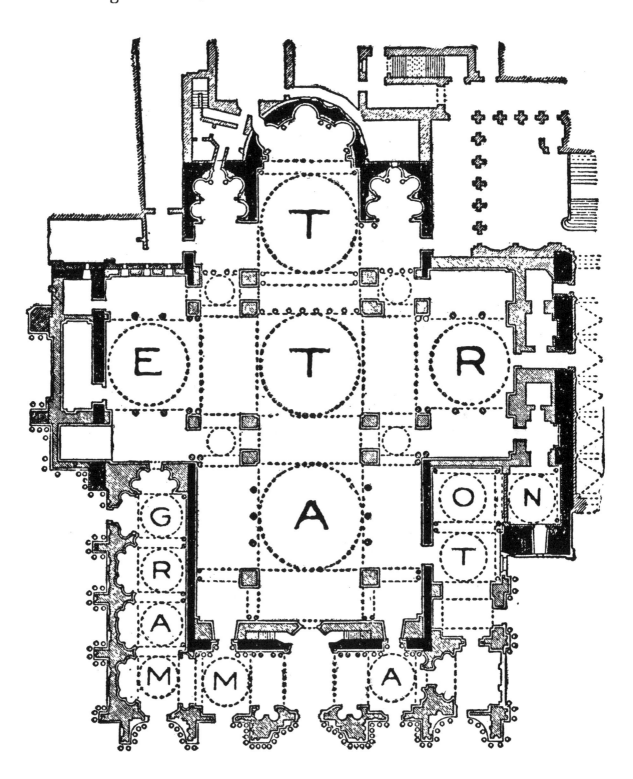

Another Riddle for Magical Thinking

Here is another ancient riddle of wizardry. Pondering it will further develop your magical thinking:

> Though learning has fed me,
> I know not a letter.
> I live among books,
> Yet am never the better.
> Each spell I digest,
> Yet I know not a line.
> What, wizard, I am,
> I beg you'll divine.

Here's a hint: the answer contains a W or M.
Here's a second hint: it is a thief in darkness.
Here's a third hint: in Old English, its name means "dragon."
Turn the page when you're ready to check your answer.

The answer is the larva of the wood-boring beetle that feeds upon paper and paste, affectionately known as the *bookworm*. Yes, our hint hid the answer in plain sight: "W or M" spells *worm*. The *wyrm* of Old English means *dragon* as well as *bug*.

Though the riddle places them in a rather bad light, bookworms are actually "walking encyclopedias," stuffed full of information but lacking the wisdom to make sense of it. When you encounter a bookworm, why not take a moment to introduce yourself and politely ask it to share what it has seen. The worm won't understand a word of what it has mindlessly taken in, but it can mechanically repeat its adventures through magical lore, and you may benefit tremendously. Have a small square of adhesive paper to offer in gratitude.

By the way, obtaining information from bookworms through cunning persistence is what led to the expression, "to worm something out of." Squirming bookworms inspired another expression: when our actions are not informed by facts, we are said to "not have a leg to stand on."

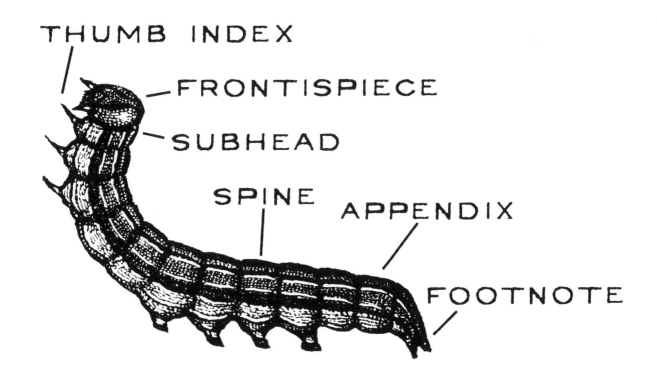

THUMB INDEX

FRONTISPIECE

SUBHEAD

SPINE   APPENDIX

FOOTNOTE

How to Write a Self-Fulfilling Prophecy

The best way to create a prediction that is bound to be correct is to scatter letters randomly into a stained-glass window. In the pattern we enclose here, a true wizard will make out the shapes of a listening rabbit, a watchful cat, a burning candle, a magical cauldron, and a walking enchanter wearing a pointed hat.

Begin with the five large hexagonal gemstones in the window. Write the vowels A, E, I, O, and U in these gemstones, in any order you wish. Give no conscious thought to the placement of letters, but rather allow your deepest all-knowing mind to play.

Then begin filling in the remaining shapes with the entire alphabet, scattered in a haphazard fashion one letter at a time. Perhaps an A will go on the cat's face; perhaps a B will go in the space above the rabbit's left ear. There is no right or wrong arrangement as long as you place each letter without thinking about it. There are enough spaces for you to scatter the entire alphabet eight times. As you come near the end of the eighth alphabet, you may find it a challenge to find the remaining spaces hiding within the stained-glass window, but rest assured that they are there and are eager to hold the final letters.

Once the window is full of letters, you will find yourself with a magnificent puzzle to ponder. Allow your eyes to dance around the window, and wait for hidden words to emerge. Any letters that touch, even at just the tips of their shapes, may form part of a larger word. Begin at the top left corner, if you wish, and see if two and then three or more letters link in any directions to form a word you recognize. As you find single words, write them down into a list.

When you feel confident that you have found most of the hidden words in the window, it is time to formulate your prophecy. The secret to making sense of your list is to begin finding pairs of related words. By way of example, we'll offer our own scattering of letters and word list. This will prove to be a rather dramatic prophecy for you, but fear not (hint: there is a very happy ending).

Here are the words we see in this window:

hits	begin	sly			
zing	sad	brag			
best	seem	lair			
bare	wee	jab			
fall	unit	vow			
rains	sting	bike			
bank	hare	lies			
sees	find	folly			
shut	clues	gate			
take	king	fee			
roll	dart	fix	dim	cry	glad
rage	shy	quell	row	in	thaw
pay	loan	sets	likes	oar	bee
key	vases	saw	hoop	jaws	pools
code	zip	unties	guts	liar	vex
luck	fund	gold	him	fall	gorilla
runs	maze	cased	six	flail	rank

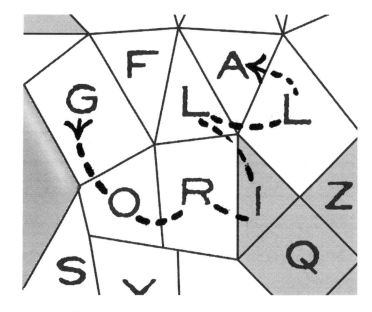

As you look over this word list, pairs begin to reveal themselves. BEE and STING go together, for example. That pair is written down so as to begin a new list. RAINS and POOLS are related, so they, too, are added to the new list. GORILLA and JAWS go together, as do SHUT and GATE, KING and GOLD, AIM and DART. As you form this new list of word pairs, you will begin to see a poem emerging.

Once you are satisfied that you have found all of the related pairs, rearrange the pairs so that they form the backbone of a story. Use additional words from the first list to flesh out your poem.

Here is the poem of word combinations that we discovered from the scattered letters in the window, followed by our interpretation. As with all prophecy, words tend to be symbolic as opposed to literal. GORILLA, for example, is not so much an actual great ape but rather a ferocious competitor.

BEE STING, VEX
SEEM SAD
CRY PINTS
RAINS POOLS
ROW OAR
GORILLA JAWS
FALL, ROLL
AIM DART, TAKE[S] GUTS
ZIP, ZING, HITS, JAB
QUELL RAGE
SEES SIX CLUES
UNTIES CODE
FIND MAZE
SHUT GATE
TAKE KEYS
HEY, WEE SHY HARE!
SLY, RUNS, LAIR
KING GOLD, BANK FUND
BEGIN SLY VOW
PAY LOAN FEE
FIX FOLLY, GLAD
BEST LUCK

The vexing BEE STING refers to a hurtful effect. Something will cause a bit of pain and annoyance. Though the distress won't be serious, you will feel hurt enough to SEEM SAD and to CRY nearly PINTS of tears, like RAINS filling POOLS. But you will be equipped to handle the sadness

193

and will, in fact, steer your way through the flood by ROWing with your trusty OAR (symbolic of whatever tool one might use to propel oneself through life's rough patches). Upon reaching dry ground, you will come face to face with the JAWS of a GORILLA—an adversary who puts up a fearsome front. You will smartly counter not with a punch, as it isn't a fairly matched fight, but rather with a defensive maneuver: FALL and ROLL. This will allow you just enough time to AIM a tranquilizer DART (which will TAKE GUTS). In other words, you will find a way to calm the aggression as opposed to battling it head-on. ZIP, ZING, your dart will HIT with an effective JAB and will QUELL the gorilla's RAGE. As you catch your breath, you will SEE SIX CLUES hidden in plain sight. Contemplating these clues, you will puzzle out a way to UNTIE the knotted CODE. You will be directed to FIND a MAZE, symbolic of a network of confusing paths that lead toward a goal. When you find the entrance to this maze, you will SHUT the GATE behind you and TAKE the KEYS. In other words, you will embark on this new endeavor and will turn your back on your former situation. However, by keeping hold of the keys, you will be empowered to return if you wish. Within the maze you will spy a WEE SHY HARE. This SLY creature will RUN to its LAIR, and in following your animal instincts you will discover the path to the repository ("BANK FUND") of the KING's GOLD. This is symbolic of whatever reward you are seeking, in the possession of an elder personage of power. You will BEGIN speaking a SLY VOW to this king, in essence sweet-talking him. You won't necessarily lie, but your promises will be carefully manipulative so as to establish your trustworthiness with the symbolic gold. Once in possession of the reward, you will be able to PAY some sort of LOAN FEE, involving something you borrowed in the past and need to reimburse. In retrospect, you will realize that the previous loan had been unnecessary, and you will be GLAD to FIX this FOLLY once and for all. Indeed, you will congratulate yourself on being gifted with the BEST of LUCK, though in truth you will have achieved all of this through your own determination and skill.

And so try your own hand at creating a self-fulfilling prophecy. This technique of decoding scattered letters in a grid will be popularized by one whose name means "Guardian of the Spear."

A Diagram for Stopping

Upon turning to this page, most readers will see one simple phrase: "This page purposefully left blank." But we wish to share a powerful diagram with you. It will put a stop, once and for all, to any action, process, or event you previously set into motion. Allow your eyes to wander around the diagram. See how many words the diagram forms, and consider why they are important.

The word STOP, naturally, brings things to a standstill. Its power is reinforced by several other words with four letters. SPOT provides a clear objective, like a target, for the magic's aim. OPTS is from the Latin meaning choosing or wishing, and it focuses your intention. TOPS places your spell uppermost in importance, as it refers to the highest degree. POTS, of course, calls upon the force of cauldrons. (And inside the cauldron? A Greek word

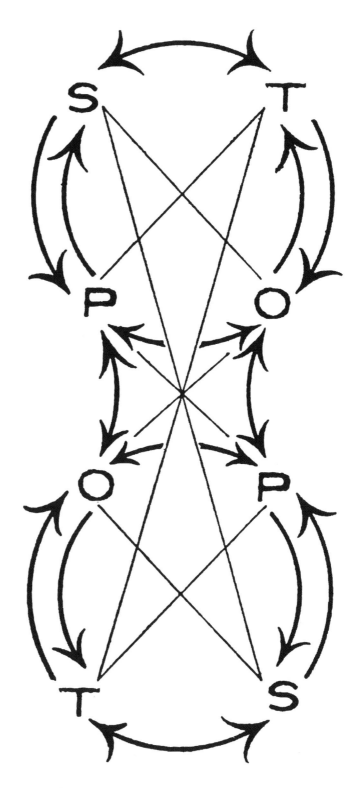

difficult to spot: OPOS, juice!) POST means both to send and with haste. POPS offers some explosive energy at the end. And TOOT is the flourish of a trumpet, marking an important event. It's true that POOP is at the center of things here, but it refers to exhaustion, not waste matter.

We cannot overlook the fact that OOPS is also present in the diagram, but it is less the possibility of failure than an acknowledgment that there is no magic incapable of being misused.

Why the Last Word is Actually the First

A Scottish philosopher will say that the eye is the first circle, the horizon which it sees is the second, and onward throughout nature circles ripple without end. The circle is therefore the highest emblem in the cipher of the world. Around every circle we can draw another, larger circle, and so on forever and ever.

A wizard's life is an apprenticeship to magic, and there is no end to learning. Every apparent finishing touch to your knowledge is actually a beginning. At the bottom of the deepest cave of wonders is a wishing well that takes us even deeper. A wizard's vital spirit tends to expand outward, embracing new spheres of interest and then bursting through those boundaries. That is because every ultimate fact of magic is merely the first of a new series.

There can be no enclosing circumference to a wizard. Ever-advancing, the wizard has all the powers of olden times yet may use them in brand new ways. A wizard carries all the energies of the darkest ages into the dawning new day, ready and eager to be surprised. A wizard never rises so high as when the destination is unknown.

And so, as you already guessed, this last word of our tome is actually the first. Such is the secret nature of things. What can we say but *Welcome!* You've opened this book at a moment when you're supposed to be doing something else. But you'll get to it later, as we both know it's something that can wait a bit. You deserve this moment to yourself, to satisfy a curiosity that has been slowly growing in the back of your mind. Relax, for we understand you.

Foreword

By Clint Marsh

Once upon a time, becoming a wizard required years of travel. The hopeful apprentice traced the contours of the known world in search of wise elders who might impart their arcane knowledge. Much of the magic the young wizard learned was based on philosophical truth concealed by clever wordplay, and the ideas of different cultures bumped up against one another in the confines of the collection. Pictograms of Chinese dragons rubbed shoulders with hieroglyphic Egyptian gods. Unpronounceable sigils—essentially squiggles distilled from potent phrases—sat smugly inside their protective circles. Arabic magic squares and Kabbalistic poems filled the margins, promising mystical secrets to anyone with the patience to unwrap them.

At the end of the tour, the apprentice returned home with a head, and perhaps a careworn notebook, brimming with charms, talismans, and incantations from around the globe—a veritable magical encyclopedia. Curled around it all might be the Norse world-serpent Jörmungandr, or perhaps its cousin the Ouroboros of Greece, a knowing snake kept silent by virtue of biting its own tail, thus binding the collection like a secret diary and uttering its secrets to no one.

Fortunately for the young wizards of today—many of them lacking the time and resources for such wondrous journeys—the ancient word-wizard Anthemion Deckle Buckram compiled the *Hexopedia*. Luckier still, modern-day mage Craig Conley has polished it up into this marvelous new edition.

Like language itself, the *Hexopedia* is a living entity. Unlike other books, however, this one is itself magical—as you read it, it reads you in return. Don't be alarmed, though. The *Hexopedia* is a conscientious telepath and a trusted companion in your work and will keep your secrets despite spilling those of the world's greatest wizards. It is also an infallible fortune-teller. Many of its prophecies have come to pass over the centuries since it was first written. And the *Hexopedia* continues its oracular trajectory with its most wonderful predictions yet, sensing your own abundant potential and encouraging you to make great strides in word magic.

What does the young wizard require in order to learn the secrets of magical words and phrases? Beyond this book itself, the needed tools are few: A brush made of goats' hair, or perhaps from the fur of a wolf. Some parchment. A bit of ink. But the wizard's most important tool is imagination. Happily, this natural resource costs nothing and, once tapped, is found to be in infinite supply. And what can be expected from such study? As you puzzle over the acrostic riddles of magic squares, gaze at written reflections, and try your hand at spelling out your own magic, you'll be breaking down, reordering, and lending power to more than just words and phrases. You'll be transforming yourself as well.

Timeless truth is often hidden in plain sight. As you'll learn leafing through the *Hexopedia,* some of the world's most powerful spells hide at the heart of the seeming nonsense of fairy tales and playground rhymes. Each exercise in these pages begins to dispel the invisibility that has been cast over countless magical lessons. To borrow the words of the magisterial Anthemion Deckle Buckram himself, "It works like a charm because it *is* a charm."

Are you ready to begin? Excellent. As with much of magical practice, the first thing you must do is suspend your disbelief. Hang it from the ceiling like a recalcitrant Ouroboros. But don't stop there. Blindfold it. Whisper questions in its ear. Spin it around and swing it back and forth. Then tickle it with the bristles of your magical brush until it gives to you its hidden truth.

Turn this truth over in your mind. Trace its words onto the page and form its phrases with your voice. Shape it into magic, and in turn let this magic begin to shape your world.

The Antiquary wishes to thank three mavens for their invaluable help in bringing lost passages of this timeless manuscript to light:

Jonathan Caws-Elwitt
William Keckler
Abigail McBride

Made in the USA
San Bernardino, CA
13 March 2017